D1341937

THE OXFORD TUTORIAL

Edited by David Palfreyman

THE OXFORD TUTORIAL:

'Thanks, you taught me how to think'

Edited by David Palfreyman

Bursar & Fellow, New College, University of Oxford
Director, OxCHEPS

With contributions from: James Clark, Richard Dawkins, Robin Lane Fox, Richard Mash, Peter Mirfield, James Panton, Roger Pearson, Penny Probert Smith, Christopher Tyerman, Alan Ryan, Suzanne Shale, Andrew Smith, and Emma Smith

This second edition published by

Oxford **C**entre for **H**igher Education **P**olicy Studies
New College,
Oxford,
OX1 3BN,
UK.
http://oxcheps.new.ox.ac.uk/

*Ox*CHEPS

Sponsored by Blackwell's, Oxford, OX1 3BQ, UK.

BLACKWELL

ISBN 978-0-9547433-7-6

This English second edition is also available on-line from the Papers Page (Item 1) at the OxCHEPS website – http://oxcheps.new.ox.ac.uk

Chinese edition, 2008, from Peking University Press, Beijing, PR China.

Printed by Aldens, Witney, Oxfordshire, OX29 OYG, UK.

CONTENTS

1. Higher Education, Liberal Education, Critical-Thinking, Academic Discourse, and the Oxford Tutorial as Sacred Cow or Pedagogical Gem

David Palfreyman, Bursar & Fellow, New College, and Director of OxCHEPS

Introduction

This Chapter explores the concept of 'higher education': just what happens in higher education and in universities that is indeed *higher* and hence different from what happens in other parts of education (schools and further/tertiary/adult education)? It suggests that *higher* education crucially means 'a liberal education', and goes on to give a selection of comments on the concept of 'liberal arts' and 'liberal education' drawn from a range of authors. The Chapter also reviews the potential conflict between the provision of liberal education and 'vocational education' within higher education, and whether the former can be incorporated into the latter – and indeed must be if the vocational education that takes place inside a university is deserving of the label *higher* education. This Chapter then explores the Oxford Tutorial as a means of delivering liberal education, itself as a process of developing critical-thinking within the context of a specialised, usually single-honours degree course – and hence not to be confused with the concept of 'general education' as the offering of a broad and mind-broadening curriculum that may well also lead to the development of critical-thinking and thus amount to a liberal education where that curriculum is taught appropriately and with adequate opportunity for the student to engage in 'academic discourse'. The Chapter concludes with a call for UK universities to rediscover the importance and value of liberal education by making amends for the short-changing of undergraduate teaching that has occurred as, over the past twenty years, the staff: student ratio has worsened and students have been steadily denied the chance properly and fully to engage in academic discourse.

What is *higher* about 'higher education'?

The first part of this Chapter asks what is *higher* about 'higher education'. Here are some thoughts…

Does *higher* education matter? What happens in *higher* education that does not happen in *primary/secondary* education (or in what was once called *elementary* education), nor in *further* education? Or is *higher* not labelling the qualitative aspect of the educational process, but merely means *tertiary*? If what goes on in HEIs is narrowly vocational in terms of teaching only 'skills' or merely involves the memorising of lecture handouts (rather than, say, also accessing books and journal articles) for regurgitation in simplistic computer-marked class-tests (rather than, say, the writing of essays – on which proper feedback, face-to-face, is given – and any other involvement in an academic discourse – within, say, seminars of up to 10/12 – and not 20/25 which can not possibly function as a practical forum for discussion), then arguably HE becomes the continuation of school: it is indeed *tertiary*, not *higher* (one might label it also as *adult education*).

Higher education, in whatever subject, is the development of the individual's communication and critical facilities (synthesis/analysis/expression) over and beyond what would have happened by the person simply getting to be 3 or 4 years older while in HE, over and beyond what comes with maturing from an 18-year old school-leaver into a 22-year old graduate employee. *And* over and beyond any knowledge corpus imparted in the degree course: the key feature is an ability to learn how to update this corpus that will unavoidably become dated. *And* over and above any technical skills also imparted in the degree course: higher education is again about knowing when and how to update those skills. *Higher* education is not 'schooling' for adults. *Higher* education is the development of critical-thinking through the process of liberal education.

Higher education is about preparing people for life-long learning and career retreading, for a life-time contribution to Society as an educated Citizen (not merely to the Economy as a Trained Worker with Skills). As such *higher* education is liberal education and goes beyond vocational education as something that is also worthy but whose remit is 'merely' to impart specific knowledge and particular skills for a defined job (plumber, hairdresser) or a predetermined career (accountancy technician, the banking exams). *Higher* education is not 'training'.

Higher education may be the starting point to a route for a set career (usually called a profession, or once a vocation (calling) – for example, medicine and the law). But it is meant to produce the reflective practitioner within such professions – the person who thinks critically about the practice of medicine or the law, who knows when and how to professionally update. (Indeed, one might have an element of liberal education within even an obviously vocational area – one might offer plumber training in such a way as to create 'the reflective plumber' rather than 'plumbing-by-numbers'.)

Admittedly, in the USA that element of the HEI involvement in the creation of medics and lawyers is left to graduate school following on from an undergraduate 'general education' or 'liberal arts education'. In the UK, in contrast, we sell law as a cheap undergraduate degree and let trainee medics loose on patients at 19/20 rather than 23/24 as in 'Scrubs' or 'ER'! And therein lies a problem – countries vary so widely in the concept of what is a degree and how long it takes to earn one, in how teaching is delivered and in how much is offered within a degree course, in how academic performance is assessed, in deciding what is quality in the teaching and learning package, and in determining what is 'graduateness' or what is fitness for purpose about higher education. US students, for example, major and minor within general undergraduate education; UK students follow a highly specialised single-honours degree course; the major continental European HE systems are somewhere between and, like the USA, take longer (while even within the UK there are differences: in England and Wales a degree course is typically three years, but four in Scotland).

Given such variation it is really rather difficult to see HE as really and demonstrably mattering in terms of promoting economic progress, as opposed to good citizenship within a liberal social democracy political model – *unless* one views its contribution to Human Capital as the development of clear communication and critical-thinking as referred to above, these being the economic value of liberal education. If it was so truly crucial in skills/vocational terms and as training for employment, one might expect HE systems in OECD countries to be more alike than they actually are as, within a global economy, they converged to match the very similar economic pressures faced by each nation. And hence, if one places the stress on such 'learning outcomes' from a first degree, then, arguably, the massification of UK HE 'on the cheap' (the unit of resource in terms of the cash to fund a year of undergraduate teaching declines over the past two decades by c40% as the student numbers double) and the resultant decline in the staff: student ratio means less teaching, less assessment, and *very much* less chance for the student properly to engage in the academic discourse. Have the 'learning outcomes' goalposts been relocated to match reduced resources (a process of dumbing-down)? Or are the expectations the same and similar outputs are achieved, despite scaled-back inputs, because the productivity of teaching and learning increases – perhaps at the expense of over-working and 'stressing-out' academics?

If the former, this means *higher* education becomes less *higher* and more *tertiary* as it shifts from a pedagogical emphasis on liberal education to a skills/curriculum dominated agenda. Ironically, Government praises such a shift as HEIs become more 'accountable' and 'relevant' to 'the world of work': in fact, the shift may be an apparent short-term gain at the expense of the longer-term benefit once got from *higher* education for Society *and* the Economy (see Moodie, 2008 forthcoming, for a comparative international analysis: liberal market economics need liberal education that better prepares graduates for rapidly changing economic conditions and related employment opportunities).

So back to the first paragraph of this section, does *higher* education matter? It probably matters less for the Economy than we in the HE industry tend to argue and than our Government paymasters like to think as they see HE through the narrow perspective of Human Capital Theory (the real economic value of HE *may* be rather more via research and technology transfer than via HCT in terms of mass under-graduate education – see Elhanan Helpman, 'The Mystery of Economic Growth', 2004). It certainly matters in the old fashioned sense of a public service for a bettering of Society, but that line of argument has not opened the Treasury money-box since the 1970s (and hence we in the HE 'industry' are defeatist and defensive in trying to justify our taxpayer-funding only in terms of the perceived/supposed economic value of HE). HE is without doubt both a positional good (credentialism in the job market) and also a consumption good (a rite of passage for the young within a rich nation that can afford to tie up the productivity capacity of half its young people in their 'benefiting' from (and, increasingly, paying for) HE until 25/26 – school to 18, a gap year, a 3/4year undergraduate degree, another gap year, a taught Masters because just everyone has a BA/BSc degree these days...). If *higher* education really is *higher*, it matters; if it is *tertiary* education, most of it should be delivered more efficiently and more economically by private commercial/for-profit providers (Phoenix, Kaplan, and others), through distance-learning, and as 'foundation degrees' taught in modest low-cost public institutions (today's FE colleges), with no nonsense about a link between *active* research and *good* teaching. *Higher* education matters only if it is liberal education that teaches people to think critically and reflectively.

And all of this stress on the broad values of liberal education (including its long-term economic benefit to both students and society) is, of course, heresy in the Brave New World of such quangoes as the Sector Skills Development Agency and in the context of the 2007 Leitch Report demanding that HE 'give employers more power' over the university curriculum, where the emphasis is to be on 'the vocational relevance of qualifications', 'employability skills', and 'economically valuable skills' that will enable UK plc to 'upskill big time and in quick time' (see *Times Higher*, 14/12/07, p 13 for the source of this depressingly simplistic jargon): we will end up with 'the training university' as a UK version of the US community college!

What is 'Liberal Education'?

The second part of this Chapter considers what various authors have said about liberal education…

Allan Bloom on 'the adventure of a liberal education', as 'the charmed years' at university which give 'the student the sense that learning must and can be both synoptic and precise' and which 'feeds the student's love of truth and passion to live a good life'. ('The Closing of the American Mind', 1987, pp 336-347.)

Gordon Graham on 'the distinguishing mark of liberal arts and pure sciences' as being 'to enrich the mind' as in turn where 'the rationale of university education properly so called lies' and where 'liberal education embellishes the technical and technological to create the professional' in subjects such as law, medicine and engineering. ('Universities: The Recovery of an Idea', 2002, pp 40-45.)

Michael Oakeshott on 'liberal learning' as 'learning to respond to the invitations of the great intellectual adventures in which human beings have come to display their various understandings of the world and of themselves' – 'the invitation to disentangle oneself, for a time, from the urgencies of the here and now and to listen to the conversation in which human beings forever seek to understand themselves'. And this activity or process takes place in a university as a place where the undergraduate 'has the opportunity of education in conversation with his teachers, his fellows and himself' and where such education there is 'the gift of an interval' in that person's life during which 'to taste the mystery without the necessity of at once seeking a solution'. If successful, the university education puts its recipient-participant 'beyond the reach of the intellectual hooligan' and will mean the graduate has 'learned something to help him lead a more significant life' by extending 'the range of his moral sensibility' and by replacing 'the clamorous and conflicting absolutes of adolescence with something less corruptible'. University teaching is *not* about 'mere instruction'. Oakeshott warns: 'A university will have ceased to exist when its learning has degenerated into what is now called research, when its teaching has become mere instruction and occupies the whole of an undergraduate's time, and when those who came to be taught come, not in search of their intellectual fortune but with a vitality so unroused or so exhausted that they wish only to be provided with a serviceable moral and intellectual outfit; when they come with no understanding of the manners of conversation but desire only a qualification for earning a living or a certificate to let them in on the exploitation of the world'. ('The Voice of Liberal Learning: Michael Oakeshott on Education', edited by Timothy Fuller, 1989.)

Cardinal Newman and 'The Idea of a University' (1852): the role of the University is to train minds ('a real cultivation of mind'), to inculcate 'the force, the steadiness, the comprehensiveness and the versatility of intellect, the command over our own powers, the instinctive first estimate of things as they pass before us', to ensure its graduates possess 'a connected view or grasp or things; and are intellectually methodical in pursuing 'intellectual excellence'. Thus: 'A habit of mind is formed which lasts throughout life of which the attributes are freedom, equitableness, calmness, moderation, and wisdom... a philosophical habit'. And the purpose of 'a Liberal Education is not mere knowledge', 'not Learning or Acquirement, but rather, is Thought or Reason exercised upon Knowledge, or what may be called Philosophy'. Nor is 'a Liberal Education 'about the intellect being formed or sacrificed to some particular or accidental purpose, some specific trade or profession'; it is about the intellect being 'disciplined for its own sake, for the perception of its own proper object, and for its own highest culture' (and the creation of 'a healthy intellect'). Such 'training of the intellect' not only is 'best for the individual himself' but also 'best enables him to discharge his duties to society'; it is the 'training of good members of society', it is 'fitness for the world', it aimed at 'raising the intellectual tone of society, at cultivating the public mind'. (From Ian Ker, 'Newman's *Ideal of a University*', in David Smith & Anna Karin Langlow, 'The Idea of a University', 1988; and from Newman himself: see also further extracts from Newman's text as part of the Preface to the Chinese edition which is also reprinted in the English edition of this book.)

Humboldt is usually seen as fostering the research university rather than the Newman concept of the Liberal Education teaching university. It has been argued, however, that Humboldt's 1810 nine page memorandum for the new University of Berlin contends that, were a university to focus only on meeting the short-term needs of the State, it would ultimately fail both the State and itself – the vocational approach to education will have crowded out long-term value. Moreover, it has been suggested that Humboldt would promote 'Education based on Scholarship', seeing the difference between school and university, between primary/secondary education and *higher* education, as being that the former is about teaching already accepted and conventional knowledge while the latter's concept of scholarship is all about the frontiers of knowledge and concentration on problems that are not yet solved: 'the teacher is then not there for the sake of the student, but both have their justification in the service of scholarship' (from Humboldt's 1810 note). This Bildung durch Wissenschaft approach within *higher* education applies equally to university research *and* to undergraduate teaching.

And while in the nineteenth century, consider **John Stuart Mill** discussing the purpose of universities when becoming Rector of St Andrew's University in 1867: 'They [universities] are not intended to teach the knowledge required to fit men for some special mode of gaining their livelihood. Their object is not to make skilful lawyers or physicians, but capable and cultivated human beings... Education makes a man a more intelligent shoemaker, but not by teaching him how to make shoes: it does so by the mental exercise it gives.'

Leo Strauss defined liberal education as 'a counterpoison to mass culture'; as 'a training in the highest forms of modesty, not to say of humility'; yet also it demands 'a boldness implied in the resolve to regard the accepted views as mere opinions': in essence, 'Liberal education is liberation from vulgarity'. ('Academic Questions', 17 (Winter, 2003/04), 31-36: reprinting a 1959 address at the University of Chicago.)

A.N. Whitehead on 'the justification for a university' as an entity that 'preserves the connection between knowledge and the zest of life, by inviting the young and the old in the imaginative consideration of learning'. Thus, the university imparts information, but it does go 'imaginatively': 'Fools act on imagination without knowledge; pedants act on knowledge without imagination. The task of a university is to weld together imagination and experience'. The undergraduate gets space and time, is 'free to think rightly and wrongly, and free to appreciate the variousness of the universe undisturbed by its perils'. The university imparts 'the imaginative acquisition of knowledge... A university is imaginative or it is nothing – at least nothing useful'. And: 'The learned and imaginative life is a way of living, and is not an article of commerce'. Moreover, 'it is quite easy to produce a faculty [academic labour force] entirely unfit – a faculty of very efficient pedants and dullards. The general public will only detect the difference after the university has stunted the promise of youth for scores of years'! Hence a real university is not to be managed as if it were 'a business organisation': 'the heart of the matter lies beyond all regulation'. ('The Aims of Education and Other Essays', 1932, Chapter VII.)

Alan Ryan: in liberal education 'the liberal ideal is political; it looks to the creation of good citizens, and in embracing liberal education as a means to an end, it looks to the education of autonomous, argumentative, and tough-minded individuals as the safest and best way of creating good liberal citizens' (and over and beyond also producing citizens 'able to survive economically'). Moreover, 'liberal education is defined less by its content than by its purpose: the provision of a general intellectual training. This plainly requires a nice balance between the absorption of information and the acquisition of the appropriate skills to use this information... a liberal education ought to inculcate both a respect for facts and some scepticism about the reliability of what is commonly taken to be fact'. Ryan later adds, in discussing campus academic free speech and political correctness: 'If you don't like having your beliefs questioned, don't go to college...'. ('Liberal Anxieties and Liberal Education', 1998.)

Alan Ryan again: 'A liberal education is not of its nature non-vocational... Recent governments have become obsessed with transferable skills; a liberal education provides them under another name, and always has done... the ability to read exactly and absorb information swiftly... the ability to speak and write coherently and directly... the ability to see the implications of numerical data and to elicit them from different presentations... [all of which is an education] that provides a broad-gauge capacity for employment'. But, at the same time, liberal education gives 'the strongest possible sense that the world is genuinely there to be enjoyed... liberal education is an education in intellectual freedom [that also imbues] a respect for scholarship'. ('A Liberal Education: and that includes the Sciences!', the next Chapter in this book...)

George Turnbull ('Observations upon Liberal Education', 1742) is the Scottish Enlightenment's version of John Locke's 'Some Thoughts Concerning Education' (1693) and Rousseau's 'Emile, or On Education'. The emphasis is on reforming schools (changes in the teaching style and a much broader curriculum) so as to educate children in a way that inculcates the personal moral responsibility of 'Young Gentlemen' for living properly within a free society that has an appropriate 'love of liberty' as 'a passion that ought not to be crushed but cherished', with 'youth' being duly 'warned and armed against the vices and snares with which they will find the world to abound as soon as they enter upon it'. Turnbull praises 'The Socratic method of teaching' where the young are encouraged 'in finding out truths by themselves': '... teachers of youth must not trust entirely to their grave and formal lectures, but take frequent opportunities of instructing their pupils by conversation... by leading them to ask questions... by acting the midwife to their thoughts... Youth, whatever science [subject, discipline] they are taught, ought to be inured to speak out what they have learned, not by rote, in consequence of serviley mandating what they have read, but easily and in their own words, from their judgements and not from their memories...'. Turnbull ranks the development of 'judgements' and 'inventions' (innovative thinking) well above 'memories' (rote learning). Thus, for Turnbull, liberal education inculcates 'the character of the deliberate judicious man... the considerate temper, or the habit of comparing and computing... patience of thinking, or the deliberative habit... an attentive thinking habit... the habit of deliberating and computing... virtue or strength of mind... habit of acting with judgement..': and all of this leaves the properly educated individual 'able to resist all the most inviting specious promises and solicitations of objects til their pretensions have been thoroughly tried and canvassed'.

Obadiah Walker ('Of Education, especially of Young Gentlemen', 1673) commends judgement 'which subtilly compareth, and accurately discerns between things that are like... the deliberate weighing and comparing of one subject, one appearance, one reason, with another; thereby to discern and chuse true from false, good from bad, and more true and good from lesser...'. It is crucial also 'to discourse pertinently and rationally' in a way that 'brings a question to a point, and discovers the very center and knot of the difficulty... [that] warms and activates the spirit in the search of truth, excites notions'. Moreover, true learning is not about 'memory' but is about the ability 'to digest what is read, and to be able to know where a difficulty lies, and how to solve it... [to] discourse, doubt, argue upon and against...'.

William Baldwin & Thomas Palfreyman in a section entitled 'Of learning and knowledge' from their 'A treatyce on morall philosophy' (1575) offer a reference to Socrates seeing himself as 'a midwife', as bringing out or bringing forth wisdom through education as a process of drawing out rather than filling up the mind; they also quote Senaca: 'Searche for the cause of everythinge' and 'An opinion wythoute learnynge cannot be good'. Plato is cited: 'As a captaine is a director of an whole boate, so reason joyned with knowledge, is the guide of life'.

Paul Axelrod: ('Values in Conflict: The University, the Marketplace, and the Trials of Liberal Education', 2002): 'liberal education in the university refers to activities that are designed to cultivate intellectual creativity, autonomy, and resilience; critical thinking; a combination of intellectual breadth and specialised knowledge; the comprehension of tolerance of diverse ideas and experiences; informal participation in community life; and effective communication skills'.

Abraham Flexner: 'The sort of easy rubbish which may be counted towards an A.B degree or the so-called combined degrees passes the limits of credibility. Education – college education, liberal education, call it what you will – should, one might suppose, concern itself primarily during adolescence and early manhood and womanhood with the liberation, organisation, and direction of power and intelligence, with the development of taste, with *culture* [original emphasis]...' ('Universities: American, English, German', 1930.)

Jorge Dominguez: 'a liberal education is what remains after you have forgotten the facts that were learned while becoming educated'. (Dominguez, paraphrasing White-head (see above) and himself paraphrased by Harry Lewis, 'Excellence Without a Soul: How a Great University [Harvard] forgot Education', 2006, p. xiv.)

Leon Botstein on US undergraduate education as 'the last link in the chain of general education, where the purposes of education legitimately reach beyond the narrow but crucial objective of preparing a young person for work and employment. Under-graduate vocational programmes fail to capitalize on this opportunity and spend too much time in technical training that quickly becomes obsolete... [when what is needed is courses that] are not narrowly utilitarian and stress skills of reasoning and inquiry that emerge from an encounter with discrete fields of study... Learning for its own sake is the best preparation for functioning competitively and creatively...'. ('Jefferson's Children', 1997.)

Derek Bok: 'As time goes by, the technical and practical skills that vocational majors learn in college become less important to continued success [in the workplace]. Such abilities as communication skills, human relations, creativity, and 'big picture thinking' matter more. Since liberal arts faculties appear to do a better job than their vocational colleagues in fostering these qualities, graduates with traditional Arts and Sciences majors begin to gain ground...'. And the corporate world faces 'faster change, more frequent career shifts, increasingly diverse workforces, and expending global operations, all of which favour a broad liberal arts education'. ('Our Under-achieving Colleges: A Candid Look at How Much Students Learn and Why They Should Be Learning More', 2006.)

George Fallis ('Multiversities, Ideas, and Democracy', 2007): 'For Socrates, liberal learning emerged through sceptical questioning, through the application of reason, and through dialogue. All our knowledge, all our ways of seeing and of doing, both individual and collective, should be subjected to the scrutiny of reason. Through civil dialogue, question-and-answer, give-and-take, true knowledge emerges. Students should challenge orthodoxy and tradition; students should not accept thoughts, rather they should have responsibility for their thoughts.' Fallis also laments the neglect of undergraduate education within the modern university, and especially where the emphasis on research drives out a commitment to teaching: 'The urgent task for the multiversity is to renew its commitment to liberal education'. He calls for the modern sprawling university ('the multiversity') to reverse the trend for 'the research mission' to devalue or even eclipse the teaching of undergraduates ('the low priority given to undergraduate study'), noting how once undergraduate education had indeed been 'the central task' or 'the pre-eminent task' as represented by the concept of the Oxford college living on 'in the Anglo-American imagination, elusively telling us what an undergraduate education *ought* to be... as a benchmark in Anglo-American discussions of undergraduate learning'. And that such 'undergraduate learning' must take the form of 'liberal learning' defined as 'not so much about the subjects studied, as it is about the spirit in which the study is conducted' (liberal education as a pedagogical process rather than liberal education or general education as a curriculum: 'Any curriculum can be a liberal education, provided the study is done in the proper spirit'). Fallis quotes a fellow Canadian, **Paul Axelrod** (see above), and notes that this process of liberal education amounts to what Newman in discussing the value of knowledge for its own sake saw as 'fitness for the world'. (Fallis also cites **Bruce Kimball**, 'Orators and Philosophers: A History of the Idea of Liberal Education', 1986.)

Francis Oakley ('Community of Learning: The American College and the Liberal Arts Tradition', 1992): noting the critics of US HE and their concerns over 'a debilitating balkanisation of studies in the humanities and social sciences, a ragged retreat into a congeries of competing (and often aggressively ideological) particularisms, an abandonment of the high ground of disinterested universalism', Oakley, in contrast, is optimistic about 'the strong scholarly fibre, the intellectual confidence, and the pedagogic integrity' of academics teaching at the US liberal arts colleges and universities, while still seeing the liberal arts tradition as potentially threatened by 'the vogue of tight academic specialisation' and 'the comparative incoherence of the typical undergraduate course of study today'. In defence of a liberal education, Oakley concludes: '... one must question the adequacy of educational approaches that are willing to sacrifice to short-term vocational advantage the age-old struggle for some breadth of intellectual perspective and the attainment of interpretative depth. For there can be no real coping without some richness of understanding. There can be, that is, no *ultimately* [original emphasis] practical preparation for living if it leaves one bereft of the wherewithal to comprehend one's situation from a vantage point less partial and a perspective less impoverished than that afforded by the task-oriented, means-end, functional rationality at which we so excel, which accounts for so many of our modern achievements, and which has come to dominate so very much of our day to day lives.'

Martha C. Nussbaum, ('Cultivating Humanity: A Classical Defence of Reform in Liberal Education', 1997): liberal education 'liberates the mind from the bondage of habit and custom, producing people who can function with sensitivity as citizens of the whole world... [who have] the ability to think what it might be like to be in the shoes of a person different from oneself, to be an intelligent reader of that person's story, and to understand the emotions and wishes and desires that someone so placed might have'.

Ron Barnett ('The Idea of Higher Education', 1990): Barnett seeks 'to restore the liberal idea of higher education' though what he terms 'the emancipatory concept of higher education' that focuses on 'understanding, self-reflection and self-appraisal', on *why* rather than merely *what,* on an academic *dialogue* rather than vocational *technique,* on *reflection* rather than simply action, on an educational process that stresses 'the opportunities for self-expression and critical self-reflection in dialogue with others' rather than the student experience being the passive receipt of instruction so that students are recognised 'as centres of consciousness' and as participants in a 'communicative' dialogue that, crucially, develops the student's 'critical abilities'. Thus, Higher Education is a process of 'cognitive self-empowerment' as the student reaches 'a state of intellectual independence', but such a liberal education view of HE is threatened by 'the double undermining' of 'an undue disciplinary narrowness' within the university and externally in the wider society by 'the narrowness of an industry-led competence-based curriculum'. Higher Education is long-term 'liber- ation' not short-term instrumentalism if it deserves to be *higher* education: as Barnett comments, 'An educational process can be termed higher education when the student is carried on to levels of reasoning which make possible critical reflection on his or her experiences... These levels of reasoning and reflection are 'higher', because they enable the student to take a view (from above, as it were) of what has been learned. Simply, 'higher education' resides in the higher-order states of mind.' Hence also, 'An institution of higher education justifies the title [only] when it fosters educational processes of the appropriate kind' – 'a deep understanding' of a knowledge area; 'a radical critique' of that area; 'a developing competence to conduct that critique in the company of others'; an element of independent inquiry by way of 'involvement in determining the shape and direction of that critique'; self- reflection', 'self-insight' and 'self-evaluation' as the student critically assesses his/her educational progress; and scope for the student 'to engage in that inquiry in a process of open dialogue and cooperation'. In short, *higher* education is not 'a sub-set of general educational ideas', nor is it *further* education in the sense of 'simply more of what has gone before'; it is *higher education* only when 'additional processes' take place over and above education, processes that are 'special' in terms of both what happens and how, and also in terms of their value to the personal development of the student and to Society (including the Economy) through 'sharing a common but critical discourse over ends, values and achievements' within a rational society. And so Barnett neatly takes us full circle back to the earlier section of this Chapter and the question of what is *higher* about 'higher education'...

The US **Webster's Dictionary** gives us: 'liberal arts – the studies (as language, philosophy, mathematics, history, literature, or abstract science) in a college or university intended to provide chiefly general knowledge and to develop the general intellectual capacities' (cf 'vocational – concerned with choice of or training in a skill or trade to be pursued as a career').

The **Oxford English Dictionary** provides us with: 'liberal – Originally, the distinctive epithet of those 'arts' or 'sciences' that were considered 'worthy of a free man'; opposed to servile or mechanical… Directed to general intellectual enlargement and refinement; not narrowly restricted to the requirements of technical or professional training' (cf 'vocational – Of, pertaining or relating to, a vocation or occupation' – citing '1979 *Yale Alumni Mag.* Apr 12/2 Of all the areas in colleges and universities that will feel… the growing vocationalism of the young, the humanities will be hardest hit…').

It will be appreciated that a couple of these gobbets date from as early as the seventeenth-century (Walker, 1673) or even earlier (Baldwin & Palfreyman, 1575): these beginnings of the Oxford Tutorial are explored by M. Feingold ('The Humanities' in N. Tyacke, 'The History of the University of Oxford: Volume IV, Seventeenth-Century Oxford', 1997) who argues that a more wide-ranging and free-thinking humanistic undergraduate curriculum replaced the over-systematised rigidity of medieval scholasticism, and that the Oxford tutor evolved as 'more to guide and supervise than to teach… the tutor assumed the role of director of studies, overseeing the [student's] more or less independent consolidation of higher-level skills'. He cites Richard Holdsworth's early-seventeenth century directions to undergraduates: 'you will finde more content, and better retain that which you get out of your own industrie, than which you receive from your tutor'. Thus, the concept developed that the BA taught students how to learn for themselves, and they then 'earned' the MA over another three years or so by continuing with their self-directed studies: as Feingold puts it, 'establishing early the habit of independent study as the key to a lifetime of learning'. But also, from Holdsworth and other seventeenth-century 'guides' to undergraduate study cited by Feingold, it is clear that the Oxford undergraduate had first to properly understand before tentatively evaluating, that the student was to be led through knowledge and learning before reaching judgement – here one is struck by the Confucian emphasis on understanding before evaluating discussed in the Preface to the Chinese edition of this text.

The Oxford Tutorial: Sacred Cow or Pedagogical Gem?

What an Oxford tutor does is to get a little group of students together and smoke at them. Men who have been systematically smoked at for four years turn into ripe scholars... A well-smoked man speaks and writes English with a grace that can be acquired in no other way.

Stephen Leacock, *My Discovery of England* (1921)

The best tutorials are like 'Newsnight' with the tutor as Paxman.

A 1990s Oxford Undergraduate (see Chapter 13)

The Oxford Tutorial has an almost mystic, cult status. It is Oxford's 'premium product' for which, via college academic fees, it commands 'a premium price'. But the Tutorial has its critics, both within and beyond Oxford. Is it an anachronism in the mass higher education system of the twenty-first century? Is the traditional tutoring of Oxford's undergraduates now too labour intensive and too expensive a burden for the University and its colleges as State funding of higher education declines? Do the dons want to escape the heavy burden of twelve hours per week of tutorial teaching and redirect valuable time into research as the key factor in achieving the plaudits of a successful academic career? Is the Tutorial a sacred cow to which Oxford pays mere lip-service as it quietly shifts to 'small group teaching'?

Or is it a pedagogical gem, the jewel in Oxford's crown, to be preserved at all costs as the best way to challenge, stimulate and truly educate Oxford's high-quality 'young' in the crucial 'lifelong-learning' skill of sound analysis and critical thinking? If Oxford lets the Tutorial wither, will it be failing future generations of talented undergraduates who need the intensity of the demanding tutorial teaching method-ology to ensure their intellectual resources best serve them in their careers and in turn Society? Moreover, how does the Oxford Tutorial fit with the concept of a Liberal Education, and anyway just what is *higher* education?

This little book brings together experienced Oxford Dons from across the academic disciplines who discuss their personal belief in and commitment to the Tutorial as an utterly *essential* element in *all* Oxford's degree subjects. It is hoped that students new to Oxford will find these essays helpful in sharing with them, as 'the consumers', what the Dons, as 'the producers', are trying to achieve, while stressing that the whole process is both 'a team effort' and also one that is *not* fixed in format since it allows tutor and tutee to vary the nature of the Tutorial to optimal effect. Thus, it can be at the same time a process which falls apart if either undergraduate or teacher short-changes the tutorial experience. Yet, as the sometime President of Magdalen College, Oxford, noted when reviewing the 2001 first edition of this book in the *Times Higher* (13/9/02, p 23): 'the tutorial is renewed, flexible, dynamic and popular' (and he added, 'even though this news often appears unwelcome to our national educational bureau-cracy'!).

The sub-title ('Thanks, you taught me how to think') comes from a former student writing to one of our Contributors after achieving a good degree result. An American student similarly wrote to me: 'You taught me how to not only research and support my arguments but also how to present them and respond to questions thoroughly and thoughtfully... It's funny, I often think of the book you handed me to read on the day of our initial meeting and the boy who said 'thank you, you taught me how to think.' I couldn't agree more. The Oxford tutorial system... was without question the most academically and personally enriching experience of my life. Thank you'.

And another American (Mallinson, 1941) commented way back: 'The pupil has the advantage of intimate contact with a good mind and a greater wisdom than his own. The tutorial prevents him from following false and valueless trails, from being overimpressed by big names and the printed word. It teaches him to examine evidence and to think for himself. When he leaves Oxford, he is probably less stuffed with facts than the graduate of any European or American University, but he should have cultivated what is the greatest essential of these times: the critical spirit. No system has ever been devised which can develop this faculty better than the Oxford tutorial. There are plenty of critics of this Oxford method, but there exists nothing else like it for discouraging authorisation and docility in learning.' The very special nature of the Oxford tutorial has attracted more recent attention in the USA, being the focus of a conference for Liberal Arts colleges on Liberal Education held at Lawrence University (Wisconsin) in 2007 and one on critical-thinking due in 2008 (as it happens here at New College in Oxford: www.criticalthinking.org); and also in China where I gave a Paper on Liberal Education at the 2007 Beijing Forum (and subsequently Peking University Press has published a Chinese edition of this text the Preface to which is reprinted in the 2008 English edition).

The Editor and the Contributors are grateful to *Blackwell's*, the justly world-famous landmark Oxford bookshop since 1879, for support in the production and distribution of the 2001 first edition and again for the 2008 second edition of this book, which pays due tribute to another special feature of Oxford in the form of the tutorial as the trademark of the University and its colleges. We are also pleased that this Oxford book has been printed by the Alden Group as another historic local business dating from 1832.

THE JEWEL IN THE CROWN?

Over the last hundred years, the tutorial teaching system has been praised as Oxford's jewel in the crown. In 1909 Lord Curzon, as Chancellor of the University, declared: 'If there is any product of which Oxford has special reason to be proud, which has stamped its mark on the lives and characters of generations of men, and has excited the outspoken envy of other nations, it is that wonderful growth of personal tuition which has sprung up in our midst almost unawares.' (Curzon, 1909, p 122)

Then the 1922 Royal Commission on Oxford and Cambridge Universities saw the tutorial embedded within the collegiate university as Oxford's (and Cambridge's) key feature:

'With all its characteristic difficulties, drawbacks and exceptions, which are on the increase, the system of College instruction is largely accountable for the educational achievement of the two senior Universities. The teaching of the undergraduate, man to man, by his Tutor or Supervisor... gives to the education at Oxford and Cambridge something scarcely to be got elsewhere in such full measure. The rudiments of the system existed in the worst days of "old corruption", increased with the growing efficiency of the Colleges in the early nineteenth century, and were brought to perfection in Balliol by the example and influence of Jowett. The system became general in Oxford and subsequently in Cambridge... But there is still a certain difference of view between Oxford and Cambridge as to the amount of individual teaching which should be given to each undergraduate, and the amount of time which academical teachers should be expected to give to this function, at the expense of time for forwarding the growth of new thought and knowledge ['research' in modern jargon!]. So far there is a difference of point of view – and it must not be exaggerated – Cambridge ideas are naturally coloured to a large extent by the experience of Science, Oxford ideas by the experiences of "Greats". Without attempting to adjudicate in so nice a controversy, we may point out the indisputable fact that great sacrifices are made by College teachers at both Universities to the personal education of the undergraduate, and that for this reason there is pressing need of the further endowment and encouragement of research... It is interesting to note that, whereas the earlier Royal Commissions [in the 1850s and 1870s] were concerned with providing against the indifference and want of conscientiousness of some of the Fellows, the charge now made in some quarters is that the Fellows overwork themselves at teaching and administration. However this may be, they have their reward in supplying the country with a system of higher instruction which perhaps gives more attention to the individual student than is given anywhere else. If complaint is made that education at Oxford and Cambridge costs more per man than elsewhere, one reason is that the undergraduate gets more teaching in return for his money, over and above the peculiar residential advantages.' (Royal Commission, 1922, pp 38/39; on nineteenth century Oxford and the emergence of the tutorial system see Engel (1983) and Brock & Curthoys (2000, pp 133-137); for an analysis of college teaching in the medieval university, and especially the pioneering role of William of Wykeham's New College from 1379, see Chapter 5 of Cobban, 1986 and Cobban, 1999; on colleges in the twentieth century see Harrison, 1994, Chapters 4 and 8; and on attempts to transplant the collegiate tradition within Harvard, Yale and Princeton see Duke, 1996, and Ryan, 2001.)

In 1964 Rose & Ziman noted, less effusively:

'Oxford and Cambridge are the most famous universities in the English-speaking world. In particular they are the most famous *teaching* universities. They are supposed to possess some special and unique method for getting intellects to sparkle, for filling heads with knowledge, for making undergraduates big with wisdom.' (Rose & Ziman, 1964, p 59)

The 1966 Franks Commission on the running of the University provided a powerful endorsement of the tutorial:

'At its heart is a theory of teaching young men and women to think for themselves. The undergraduate is sent off to forage for himself... and to produce a coherent exposition of his ideas on the subject set... In [the tutorial] discussion the undergraduate should benefit by struggling to defend the positions he has taken up...' (pp 101-2)

Similarly, the 1997 North Report repeated the mantra:

'...[the tutorial system] encourages the student to take an active rather than passive role in learning and develops skills in self-directed study and working independently, as well as analytical and critical skills', and, moreover, it provides the undergraduate with 'the opportunity to discuss particular topics in considerable detail with the tutor, who may well be a leading expert in the subject or a young active researcher at the forefront of the discipline' (pp 163-4; on twentieth century Oxford generally see Harrison, 1994.)

THE JEWEL ANALYSED

Yet the only detailed assessment of the true worth of the tutorial system dates back to the 1960s, when Will G. Moore, Fellow and Tutor of St John's College, published in 1968 *The Tutorial System and its Future*. Moore describes what a tutorial is:

'At its most simple the tutorial is a weekly meeting of the student with the teacher to whom he is especially committed. This does not replace other methods, such as instruction by lecture or in class. It clearly cannot replace private study. Indeed, it assumes all these, and includes their results in the preparation of a weekly essay, which is presented orally, listened to by the tutor and discussed immediately. The whole process – of reading, discussion, arrangements for the following week – takes up little more than an hour.

A usual feature of the method is informality... It opens with a few questions as to how the student has "got on" with his subject and a brief confession on his part, perhaps that he liked it better than he expected to, or that he was conscious that he had not covered the ground nor uncovered the real problem within the subject. Then the reading, interrupted at will by the tutor, and at times by the student, followed by perfunctory praise or thanks and then by detailed comments, which the student is free to take down or not as he prefers. This part can be either free interchange of points or painfully one-sided information. The final minutes are devoted to suggestions and hints about next week's subject and the session ends when the next pupil knocks on the tutor's door or when the first pupil departs to a lecture or the tutor to a meeting, or, indeed, when either side feels that the other is losing interest.

Not all tutorials are like this. As in other living forms of education, the norm is not the rule. Endless variations are possible, and are, indeed, produced by circumstances. Two, or even three, pupils may be present; one will be asked to read and the other to hand in his essay. A busy tutor may ask for a summary of the main points of two or three essays, weaving them into a single discussion. Either side may refuse to play its traditional part: the pupil may bring no essay, or one not his own; he may rely on confession, of failure, of interruption ("parent crisis" said one once), of illness. The tutor may bypass discussion for analysis, of documents, of problems. He may be tempted by the astute pupil into defence of his own writings. A single hour may be inadequate for a lively or complicated discussion. Some tutors "run over", getting later as the morning wears on; others leave two or more hours free for the good performers. I have dismissed bored pupils after 50 minutes and, at the other end of the scale, a philosophy tutorial starting at noon may well not finish until college lunch is over.' (pp 15/16)

Moore recognises that the Tutorial is not readily subject to, in the modern jargon, 'quality control':

'What happens in a tutorial depends so much on the two or three personalities taking part in the exercise that the keynote is variety: almost anything may happen. A colleague looking in on a neighbour's tutorial found that nothing at all seemed to be happening, and concluded that both parties were asleep. The picture of an undergraduate being "smoked at" by a laconic and occasionally oracular tutor may be true, but it is not typical, for many other pictures would be no less true. Students vary, especially when on their own: some pretend to be stupid, some are stupid, some are lazy and plausible, some are easily discouraged, few work well without praise, many conceal their real attitudes, not many are able to help the tutor to be both clear and interesting. Teachers vary no less, and any good teacher will vary his tactic. Not many of us, I think, manage to be both concise and interesting. There are times to be cryptic, and to be plain, to be sarcastic, and to be sympathetic, to expatiate and to hint. Experience has taught me that, whatever the tactic, one's best formulae may fall on deaf ears, and one's inanities may be remembered. Reception of wisdom seems to have less to do with the wisdom than with the sense on the part of the disciple that he can contribute, that his role is not to be eternally told things he must accept...

The tutor is not a teacher in the usual sense: it is not his job to convey information. The student should find for himself the information. The teacher acts as constructive critic, helping him to sort it out, to *try* it out sometimes, in the sense of exploring a possible avenue, rejecting one approach in favour of another. The whole process turns around the concept of bias: how you see things, how you evaluate evidence, how you tend to connect one fact with another. The student soon learns the teacher's mind, that a certain teacher tends to apply certain criteria or to favour certain types of evidence. From this point onwards the good student will acquire independence of his teacher, will grope after his own means of interpretation. The good teacher will thus help the student to refute or correct him, which is to say that he will teach method rather than hard and fast conclusions. The great temptation of the teacher is to cling to particular interpretations of evidence. It is hard for us to learn that our students may find their feet in using our methods to reject our views.

Here I think we touch the nerve of power of the tutorial as a tool of learning. Each side is free to refuse what is offered by the other. This may (and does) mean waste of time and effort, boredom and sense of frustration, on both sides.' (p18)

Moore sums it all up as follows:

'Here, I suggest, are the roots of the tutorial method. It is a sceptical method, a method that inquires, probes, scrutinises. It is not at its best in *ex cathedra* authoritative statement, but in criticism, theory, analysis, comparison. It prefers the relative to the absolute, the tentative to the dogmatic, the essay to the treatise. Obviously – and this we must consider later – it is antagonistic too much in the modern temper and does not offer that certainty which the young so often and so naturally seek. A university in which the tutorial method operates is not likely to offer a blueprint for society, to speak with the voice of authority, to fix, determine, assert, sanction, denounce. It is rather a university seeking to be the one place in society where inquiry may proceed without regard to the consequences, where theory may clash with theory, to be the home of point and counterpoint, of dialectic rather then of dogma.' (pp 31/32)

Finally, Moore ends his little book by quoting a colleague (Dr Marjorie Reeves, Vice-Principal of St Anne's College, giving evidence to the Franks Commission):

'When every effort has been made to make instruction effective... it is still true that there is no substitute for the individual tutorial, either singly or in pairs. Its function is *not* to instruct: it is to set the student the task of expressing his thought articulately, and then to assist him in subjecting his creation to critical examination and reconstructing it. The charge of spoon-feeding so often levelled against the tutorial method implies a complete misunderstanding of its function: it should be the most adult relationship between teacher and student, not the least... Unless all [other teaching methods] lead towards tutorial work, the final and essential stage in education may never be reached. This is the process of handling material for oneself and of bringing together one's own analysis, reflection, judgement in a form which is really a creation of individual thought. No one will dispute that this is the crown of the educational process. What is not so fully accepted is that the very production of an essay by a student demands that it should be subjected to detailed, individual criticism, otherwise his educators have failed him at the last.' (pp 65/66)

BUT IS THE JEWEL NOW PASTE?

Ted Tapper and I ask (and answer) this question in our *Oxford and the Decline of the Collegiate Tradition*:

'...Will Oxbridge be able to sustain its pedagogical exceptionalism? ...[will] the remaining exceptionalism simply melt away to survive only as one of Oxbridge's myths? At present the jewel in the crown may be smaller and more flawed than it once was, but it is not paste – or least, not yet.' (p 124). We recognise the financial pressures pushing the University and its colleges away from the one: two model of the tutorial towards 'small group teaching'. There is also the reluctance of some academics to devote so much time to their 'tutorial stint' or to give tutorials in areas of the academic discipline not of research interest to them: on the duty of the academic profession to achieve a fair balancing of teaching and research see Kennedy, 1997; and note general concerns that teaching is being progressively short-changed in the heavily research-oriented culture increasingly dominant within some institutions. Perhaps at Oxford such an undesirable shift is less likely given that the prime, even sole, function of the colleges is to be undergraduate teaching institutions, while the University worries about balancing *its* resources between teaching and research. In short, a powerful federal model of the robust USA kind advocated by Siedentop (2000) for the evolution of the EU: '...federalism is a political system which makes it possible to combine the advantages of small states [the Oxford colleges] and of large states [the University itself], without at least some of the disadvantages attaching to each.' (p.26).

Thus we also comment:

'...all the evidence demonstrates that we have a mixed pattern of teaching at Oxbridge; a combination of tutorials, lectures, demonstrations and seminars/classes, much of which is under the control of the faculties rather than the colleges. It is also important to ask what are the critical elements within this mixed pattern. How really crucial for the average student are tutorials as opposed to demonstrations in the laboratory-based disciplines?... To what extent does tutorial teaching provide an interesting, and perhaps for some students (the below average or the exceptionally gifted?), a critical supplementary input into the learning process, with the core of the discipline acquired through other means? If, as is often insisted, there should be a better integration of the contrasting teaching methods, usually of lectures and tutorials, is it not likely that the tutorials will be integrated into the lecture series? If so, the tutorials could provide the forum for the analysis of issues first raised in lectures. The pattern of tutor responses to these questions is likely to be varied, although one suspects that there would be significant clusters within differing disciplines. But such questions do help to focus attention upon an assessment of the relative importance of tutorial teaching, and how important the colleges really are in any overall judgement of the varying inputs into the teaching process.' (p115)

And we conclude positively:

'The flexibility of the tutorial system has enabled it to survive; it has been continuously redefined to meet changing conditions and new demands, and, in some form or other, it will persist into the twenty-first century. But whether it will continue to be Oxbridge's 'jewel in the crown' is an entirely different matter. We have argued that in terms of structure, process and purposes college tutorials have changed, are changing and will continue to change. Therefore, whether in 20 years we have a tutorial system that is recognisable to today's students, let alone yesterday's, is debatable.' (p 122)

In doing so we note one hugely respected Tutor of 'the old school', J.R. Lucas, defending his experience of the tutorial system and stressing that the giving of good tutorials is *not* all about teaching *only* the research territory of interest to the Don:

'We do not need to know the subjects we teach – often we teach better those subjects we do not know, for then not only do we not over-burden the pupil with more information than he can assimilate, but we show him how someone starting from a position of ignorance like himself can tackle an unfamiliar problem... it is good for tutors to be generalists in their teaching, and to cover the whole of the syllabus.' (Lucas, 1996, p 5; see also Lucas, 1999, and Allison, 1998; along with Howard-Johnston, 2006.)

That said, there are critics of the Oxford tutorial; here is Felipe Fernández-Armesto writing in *The Spectator* ('Decline and Fall', 29/12/01):

'The tutorial is Oxford's hallmark: every undergraduate gets – or, in theory, should get – weekly individual attention from an accomplished scholar, who takes an interest in the young person's work, and criticises, encourages, inspires and guides it. Ideally, if you are an undergraduate willing to get the best out of your tutors, they become your friends. Nowadays, such an ideal is rarely fulfilled. Social and generational gaps yawn in the tutorial, making it tedious and unrewarding. Unlubricated by sherry, which underpaid tutors can no longer afford to splash around, the relationship never takes off. Friendly overtures are likely to be mistaken for sexual harassment.'

He continues:

'Few tutors see much of their students; overwork cuts tutorials down to the bare minimum of allotted time. Many dons remain dedicated to the old school of selflessness, but who can blame others for whom research 'productivity' makes teaching seem an irrelevant chore? The time needed to make tutorials effective is enormous, if all undergraduates are to get the individually tailored courses that they deserve. In any case, because of academic specialisation, the relationship with a single tutor is too rarely sustained. Students spend terms on end with whippersnapper graduates as their tutors, instead of the wise old masters they hoped to meet. This is fine in small doses, as some of the young have a teacher's gift that withers with age. But too often it is a source of disillusionment and a waste of time. Subject tutors, who arrange the distribution of tutorials, are devoted but harassed, because they believe in their undergraduates and feel that they deserve the best but often cannot recruit the best to teach them.'

Cartwright (2008) recognises that the tutorial system collapses if it becomes too focused on exam-passing ('...there is pressure to prepare students for exams rather than for a life of elevated thought'), but also sees its great strength: 'The tutorial system, by design or accident, is addressed directly to the questioning of received wisdom and the probing of meaning' (while at the same time having the virtue that, in a 1:2 set-up, 'no undergraduate can slip through the net without being noticed... excuses and alibis quickly find out the lazy and the evasive or reveal the troubled'). Hence Cartwright quotes the poet Louis MacNeice:

That having once been to the University of Oxford
You can never really again
Believe anything that anyone says and that of course is an asset
In a world like ours

Cartwright also notes the comments of one long-serving English Don that the Oxford Tutorial 'does not exist as in the myth, a Socratic dialogue between tutor and undergraduate... it has not really operated in that way since the seventies, the tutor tuning and tweaking the young mind. The tutorial burden and the possibility of having to spend one hour at least with an unresponsive undergraduate has led some tutors to favour [larger] classes for two hours at a time... [such] teaching is more than ever necessary, because many undergraduates arrive without having read much.' That said, Cartwright concludes: 'But the tutorial system is still a living component of the Oxford myth and a real part of the allure of Oxford... it is seen as having class, something utterly distinctive and part of the cultural capital that comes with having been at Oxford.'

OK, WHO PAYS?

How is the tutorial system still (just) affordable for Oxford (and Cambridge) when it is not financially viable at any other UK university or even at most US universities? The financial cost is mainly in maintaining a generous staff-student ratio not now to be found elsewhere. There is also a human resources cost in that Oxford Dons carry a higher teaching load than their colleagues at other 'elite' universities – and, given Oxford's success in research terms, this means (believe it or not!) that the 'labour productivity' of Oxford Dons is above average for academics in the UK HE 'industry' (and UK HE is already itself very competitive by OECD norms). The 'cost' for the Oxford student is that, when he or she compares notes with friends who have gone to other UK universities, it *may* well be that the Oxford student is being worked harder within the intensive Oxford tutorial teaching system than the sixth-form friend who has gone on to a less generously resourced university: it is, of course, ultimately for the individual Oxford tutee to decide whether that is a price worth paying!

The extra money needed to sustain the favourable Oxford staff-student ratio is partly Oxford's private charitable permanent endowment of c£2.5 billion, mainly located in the wealth of the colleges (ranging from c£150m to c£10m – see the Table in Tapper and Palfreyman, 2000, p 158, but at least double the figures for 2007/2008). It is also partly the premium tuition fees payable by Oxford students: although usually in fact paid by the UK Government on their behalf in the case of UK and EU undergraduate students. These college tuition fees amount to c£4500 pa (in 2007/08) for self-financing undergraduates (mainly non-UK/EU 'overseas' students), but the net extra each year per UK/EU undergraduate student compared with other UK universities is 'only' some £2K since there are complicated calculations which reduce the premium per UK/EU student by the time the taxpayer money reaches the colleges via the HE Funding Council and via the University centrally. In short, the Oxford undergraduate will have spent on his/her teaching, allowing for this endowment income and for these additional tuition fees, at least £5K per annum more than the student gets elsewhere, and this extra money translates mainly into the tutorial teaching experience and also into the additional library resources of Oxford compared with other universities (see OxCHEPS, 2004, as noted below). In fact, the Government money combined with college endowment is an example of, in the modern jargon, a public: private partnership ('PPP')—perhaps, indeed, even of 'The Third Way' so in vogue amongst certain politicians!

Some other UK universities can still (just?) maintain 'small-group teaching' at, say, 7-10 in a seminar, but the 'massification' of UK higher education since 1985 has seen student numbers double while annual funding per student has almost halved: the result is that in many UK universities 'seminars' may now involve up to 25 students, for whom the opportunity for *regularly and frequently* producing, submitting *and then discussing* a variety of their own written-work is correspondingly reduced compared with the intensity of student: academic interaction within the (so far) fairly unchanging Oxford tutorial teaching system. The mass UK HE system may now provide many more young people with a taste of higher education (and rightly so compared with the unduly restricted access to university in the 'expanded elite' HE system of thirty years ago), but 'massification' on the cheap has meant that 'the student experience' of today is, for some of those young people, a rather impoverished version of what was the norm for yesterday: sadly, for them the taste is of a less rich diet.

This is hardly surprising when a staff: student ratio of about 1:12 twenty years ago has since worsened everywhere except at Oxford (and Cambridge), and indeed worsened to the extent even of 1:20-plus at some universities. As already noted, the UK has acquired a mass HE system without being prepared to pay for it (UK spending on HE is half the OECD average, and little more than a third of the USA); nor, by US norms and for reasons of political dogma and timidity, requiring/allowing the middle-class student/family to pay a fair 'top-up' academic fee for the preservation of a decent level of tuition within *all* UK universities and to the benefit of *all* students. It needs to be noted that these middle-class parents have seen marginal rates of taxation reduce considerably from the levels reached in the 1960s and 1970s: but the naïve expectation has become that the paying of low US-style tax rates can buy European standards of social provision (adequately resourced health-care, schools, and policing; a safe and reliable national railway system and subway/underground in the capital city; low-fee higher education…). For an analysis of the funding of the University of Oxford and its colleges see the OxCHEPS study as Item 13 at the Papers page of the OxCHEPS web-site (the 2007/08 cost of delivering undergraduate education is well over £20,000 pa, of which not much more than £3000 pa is recovered as the tuition fee to UK/EU undergraduates). For an analysis of the importance of the tutoring element in the overall undergraduate teaching process generally in universities see Bruce Macfarlane's 'Beyond performance in teaching excellence' in Skelton (2007). For a critique of how 'clicking' replaces 'thinking' in degree courses that place too much emphasis on 'e-learning' and 'i-lectures', and also on skills and competencies agenda of supposedly vocational programmes, see Tara Brabazon (2007); and, more generally on deficiencies in higher education, see Mary Evans (2004) and Naylor (2007).

In the case of universities the effects of the steady decline in resources are manifested only slowly and in much less dramatic ways than in the case of, say, cancelled hospital operations or cancelled school lessons, and, therefore, receive virtually no public, political or media attention. That said, some students do detect that all is not well: student satisfaction surveys record only a minority of students viewing the quantum of teaching as 'very good', while a significant minority of students felt they do not get enough 'feedback' and are not being fully stretched academically. It is especially sad that such student commitment, energy and enthusiasm should not be *fully* utilised, stimulated and challenged at a time when, more than ever, a well-educated population seems crucial to social and economic success. For a discussion of the potential for a student-consumer backlash in the context of increasing tuition fees and of the student: university contract to educate, see Chapters 13 & 14 of Farrington & Palfreyman (2006).

Indeed, as Peter Scott muses in his essay in Warner & Palfreyman (2001), perhaps UK HE is still (just?) left with the culture of an 'elite' system (low student 'wastage', high-input undergraduate teaching, a decent approach to 'pastoral care'), while increasingly being obliged to operate within a 'mass' structure (in terms of a doubling of student numbers and greatly reduced levels of funding). Scott sees the UK model of HE as a unique 'hybrid mass-elite system', and speculates on whether it is 'a stable formation' or is 'merely a moment of equipoise': he concludes that there is 'no compelling evidence' to suggest that things can't go on as they are… Interestingly for our purposes, Scott comments: 'The attention paid to the 'student experience' in the British system may partly reflect a new emphasis on students as consumers and on 'customer service', but it also represents a reworking of traditional assumptions about academic intimacy, ultimately embodied in the ideal of the Oxbridge tutorial system, which seems out of place in a truly mass system.' (p 194). Thus, the Oxford Tutorial as an anachronism. This uneasy elite-mass relationship has been so far sustained on the back of the hugely increased productivity of 'the academic labour force', as referred to earlier, but, arguably, UK HE will eventually be forced to move towards European 'pile-em-high' norms or the US public-private 'mixed economy' model for HE provision (*if* the politicians will ever allow UK universities any freedom to set tuition fees within a higher education marketplace as supposedly autonomous institutions and within a model of high(ish) fees combined with high(ish) student financial aid for those needing it to ensure means-blind admission).

For more on the funding of higher education, especially comparing the UK with the USA and the tuition fee levels at US public and private universities, see Palfreyman (2004), and also Barr (2001). Indeed, as Barr comments, when discussing the 1997 *re*-imposition of university tuition fees (UK HE having been 'free' only for 20 years since 1977) and when advocating (despite the alleged immorality of charging for HE) a marketisation of UK HE with students as 'a savvy, streetwise consumer group' (p 173) paying full tuition fees in order to remove the massive State subsidy to the middle-classes: '…taxpayer subsidies [via low-interest student loans and cheap tuition] are regressive: the taxes of truck-drivers pay for the degrees of old Etonians. In my view *that* is immoral.' (p 216, original emphasis). Moreover, Barr notes that the provision of free undergraduate degrees over these 20 years has *not* done anything much to increase access to HE amongst the lowest socio-economic groups and hence that university remains a public service 'disproportionately consumed by people from better-off backgrounds' (p 180). Tuition fees for UK/EU undergraduates have, of course, since increased to c£3000 pa, and this 'cap' is due to be reviewed in 2009/10…

It remains to be seen, therefore, whether the colleges and Oxford generally are able to sustain the tutorial system for much longer, as not only the taxpayer continues a ten year retreat from paying the cost on behalf of UK/EU undergraduates, but also (as already noted) the Government 'caps' the charging of tuition fees to the UK/EU undergraduate student at the current artificially low rate. A college like New College can for the moment keep the system going by stretching the endowment yield to cover the shortfall of c£250K pa in public funding. Poorer Oxford colleges do not have the good fortune of being so well-endowed, and hence richer colleges like New College, St John's, Jesus, Queen's, Merton and Magdalen have doubled their contribution to the inter-collegiate 'College Contributions Fund' used to provide financial aid to the less well-off colleges. Thus, there will be no politically embarrassing immediate bankruptcy amongst the colleges: but, unless greater 'top-up' tuition fees are charged and/or extra endowment capital found, they will simply, slowly and collectively, sink into a steady decline as they continue to stretch Oxford's endowment over at least a third too many undergraduates (c11,000: plus c6,000 postgraduates) for it to be financially viable in the long-term in terms of sustaining the intensive teaching package and maintaining the Listed Building infrastructure.

Time will also tell whether Oxford (and Cambridge), in the absence of an ability to determine the level of tuition fees and given that neither has anywhere near the endowment assets (each at, say, £2.5 billion) of their 'Premier League' US rivals, can in the longer term remain internationally competitive in research with Harvard (at c£15b), Yale (c£8b), Princeton (c£7b, and only *half* the size of Oxford) and Stanford (c£7b), while at the same time trying to continue to offer a premium-product teaching system for undergraduates. Is the fate of the flagship(s) of UK HE to go the same way over the next few decades as, over the past twenty-five years or so, we have seen the relative decline of the NHS, the London Underground, and our railway infrastructure? Perhaps, as discussed above, nobody who matters will actually notice, still less care: those who notice, and care, *and* have the money can anyway always send their children to an Ivy League US institution as Oxford manages itself into mediocrity! As Robert Stevens, recently retired Master of Pembroke College, Oxford, wrote in *The Spectator* ('Eviscerating Oxford', 14/7/01, p 22): '...in the federal university it has been the commitment to undergraduate education by the colleges that has made Oxford distinctive and, thus far, has also kept Oxford in the league of international universities... but Oxford, along with other leading universities, will continue its genteel decline... [given] the increasing discrepancies between the Ivy League and Oxford... There is so much that is good in English higher education, and so much that is good at Oxford, but inward-looking complacency in the university, and mindless political opportunism in New Labour, may well be doing damage which will be impossible to repair.'

So, dear Fresher reader, make full use of and enjoy the Oxford Tutorial while it's still here, for you may be the last generation to benefit from its availability! Alternatively, if it survives, you may be the last generation of British students not personally paying to your college hefty tuition fees for the Oxford Tutorial experience...

AND SO?

This little book invites all those involved in the Oxford tutorial system to reflect on the pedagogical processes it enshrines, on how and why it can work well, and on how and why it can go badly wrong. All of these essays, including this Chapter 1, are written by individuals in a personal capacity: they are not the official view of College X or University Department Y; they are (thankfully for the reader!) not the product of a Colleges' Committee or of a University Working-Party. *Nor can the reader safely assume that all the contributors to this book would agree with the Editor's stance on tuition fees set out in this Chapter!* The one common theme is to open up debate on, to evaluate, and (yes) to defend the Oxford Tutorial: and especially to help those newly exposed to it to understand how it might work for them.

As an editorial entitled 'Trademark' in the *Oxford Magazine* (No. 191, Fourth Week, Trinity Term 2001) put it: 'What marks Oxford out on the map of education is the tutorial... our distinctive mark... but the structure behind the façade is getting a touch precarious...'. The editorial goes on to note that Oxford has not been good at discussing, let alone analysing and (as the examiners would demand) critically assessing, the value of the Tutorial as a pedagogical technique. The editor sums up that value, as he sees it: '...the boost to a student's self-esteem that comes from being given the floor [and which thus despatches him/her] out into the world with the confidence of those who have been listened to seriously in demanding company, though with the critical awareness too of those who have sometimes heard themselves blunder there. It gives... a zest for self-presentation... a life-long pleasure in knowing a piece of work is well prepared...'. Hence, the editor warns with respect to the Oxford Tutorial that, as the University of Oxford and its colleges talk of economies and reform in the delivery of undergraduate teaching, 'we should hesitate before we ration this ancient advanced form too strictly, or lose it to sight behind veils of theory, or rationalise it away altogether. *In hard times no one much else is likely to stock the genuine article*. That makes it doubly ours [as Oxford's 'distinctive mark'].' (emphasis added).

Similarly, Diane Purkiss, Fellow in English, Keble College and formerly Professor of English at Exeter University, also talked of student confidence when she wrote in the *Times Higher* (19/1/01, p II of a 'Student Focus' supplement): '...where does academic confidence come from? Virtually all our students [in the UK] are bright, yet many are plagued by fear... pick 'n' mix systems [of undergraduate teaching] flounder horribly in student underconfidence... They are afraid of feeling days of uncertainty before a difficult text is mastered. At Oxford, though, things are rather different... the pox of underconfidence has [not] spread here... [Why not?] First, the entire second year [at Keble] knew they would have to master *The Faerie Queene*. They knew that I would make them write an essay on it, *and rewrite the essay if it was unsatisfactory*... They knew they could not duck it [compared with a pick 'n' mix degree structure]... Second, and this is important, these [Oxford] students have incomparably more resources than students I have taught anywhere else... They have three libraries at their disposal... *They also have me for an hour a week with just two of them asking questions [in a Tutorial], instead of 25 of them [in a Seminar]. They are much more likely to identify with my aims for them this way than if they can barely see me at the end of a long table...* Third, their confidence has already received an enormous boost from the fact that they are at Oxford in the first place...' (emphasis added; see Emma Smith's Chapter 8 for more discussion specifically on the studying of English at Oxford).

Indeed, in my essay on 'The Ancient Collegiate Universities: Oxford and Cambridge' (Chapter 2 of Warner & Palfreyman, 2001) I argue that: 'Employable graduates is Oxford's key output, whatever academics may feel about the value of their research activity, in terms of the need for the University to serve society and the economy. Oxford's graduates remain immensely employable, given the mix of intelligence, motivation, achievement at school, 'social capital' networking before and while at Oxford, *and (crucially if the Oxford teaching process is to add anything to that already potent mix) of being worked hard and consistently in the intensive tutorial teaching system...*' (p 19, emphasis added). Thus, 'if higher education (like Premier League football or Olympic-level sport) is necessarily elitist, then Oxford (together with a handful of other UK elite HEIs) has the job of taking the best students (*carefully and fairly selected*) and coaching them (*in a very demanding and intensive way*) using academic staff who are themselves the best available... It would fail the talent sent to it, and in turn the nation, if it were staffed by second-rate academics on third-rate salaries, and failed to demand of those talented students less than total commitment and prolonged hard-work in order to earn the Oxford degree...'(p 20, original emphasis). And, of course: 'The tutorial is the key feature of this demanding and intensive learning experience vital to the proper use of that talent...' (p 20).

Moreover, a weekly tutorial covering progressively almost all, or even all, of the syllabus *should* mean that, since there is no place for the ill-prepared student to hide in a 1:1 or 1:2 tutorial, the vast majority of Oxford undergraduates, being (of course) conscientious, will read over the bulk of the syllabus. This *may* in turn mean that the average Oxford graduate is more widely read than his/her counterpart at some other UK universities where a less well-resourced teaching system *might* allow the student more scope to play the course assessment game by, say, concentrating only on that part of the syllabus tested in the assessed work and/or on the limited range of examination questions the student hopes to get away with preparing for! And hence, *if* this is the case, Oxford's graduates ought to be even more attractive to potential employers: they should not only be used to facing a sustained demand for frequent and regular work, but also be widely grounded in their academic discipline (in so far as any particular academic subject matters much to most recruiters of graduates over and above the generic value of attending a good-quality university for a Liberal Education – see the earlier section of this Chapter and also Chapter 2).

The future of the Oxford Tutorial is, of course, linked inextricably with Oxford as a collegiate university, and so with the survival of the Oxford colleges as legally and financially independent self-governing entities under the Oxford University federal umbrella. Certainly their future is threatened by pressures for change both internal and external to the University, and 'the nightmare scenario' is that the present organically rich diversity of the colleges as human-scale teaching and social institutions could be lost if they become mere Listed Building halls of residence inside Oxford University as an increasingly large, centralised, and dull university: a result which to some might seem more 'economical' and 'efficient', but which will be far less 'effective'. In our *Oxford and the Decline of the Collegiate Tradition* (Tapper & Palfreyman, 2000) we explore the meanings of 'collegiality' in relation to the dynamics of professional life for academics, to the structure and hierarchy of the academic department within the university as an organisation, and to the college as an academic community. We evaluate the challenges that collegiality faces in the context of a mass higher education system and public-sector 'new managerialism'. We conclude positively: the greater probability for the Oxford colleges still is of 'collegiality as colleges' adapting (as it has done for, in some cases, 600 or 700 years) and indeed flourishing within a reinvented, revitalised and robust 'vision' and 'mission' for the twenty-first century. (See also Palfreyman, 2007.)

But, whatever may happen in the longer term, the Oxford Tutorial and your college are safe enough for the next three or four years, so please make the very best of all that Oxford has to offer: sport, theatre and drama, music, student societies of every kind (even create your own!), student politics, endless late-nights putting the World to rights... But, above all, never neglect your academic work. While there is a risk that parts of UK HE may increasingly be driven to behave like yet another vast service industry, here in Oxford you are *not* merely a passive consumer of higher education; you must be an active participant in the tutorial partnership if it is to be worthy of being called *higher* education. If you fail to play your part, you fail yourself and those supporting you (parents *do* make sacrifices to get their off-spring through university, and the British taxpayer in general *is* paying c£5-15K pa, depending on the exact degree course, for you to be here), *and* perhaps worse still you are wasting a place that another young person might have been making better use of. That said, settling into Oxford (and indeed any university) can be stressful, and, for a very few, traumatic: if you experience problems, do seek help sooner rather than later by discussing and sharing your worries (Oxford colleges are strong on 'pastoral care', and even Bursars are sympathetic towards students with genuine financial difficulties!).

To help you make the best of the Oxford what follows is a series of brief essays from experienced Dons in different academic subjects sharing their understanding of what is a Tutorial, what is needed from tutor and tutee to make it a worthwhile experience for both, how it can work well, and why it sometimes fails as a teaching process. These pieces are not prescriptive of, nor detailed maps of, *exactly* what will happen to you in tutorials: they give a flavour. The great benefit of such small-scale and personal (if expensive!) teaching is that there is maximum flexibility for individual tutors, and to an extent tutees, to vary the format to optimal effect for the two or three people involved: it is tutor *and* tutee(s) *versus* University Examiners! In addition, the sometime Director of Oxford's Institute for the Advancement of University Learning contributes another short piece on how the Oxford Tutorial fits within the context of, and the theories on, higher education learning. (See also Ashwin (2005 & 2006) along with Trigwell & Ashwin (2003) who comment that Oxford students who see their tutorials as a chance to explore ideas and to enter into the academic discourse, rather than merely as a chance to get information, get better degree results: more generally see Panton, 2004.) But, first, the present Warden of New College, Alan Ryan, puts the Oxford Tutorial in the wider context of a Liberal Education (Ryan, 1998); and, appropriately, we end by reprinting an Address from a former Warden of New College, A. H. Smith, to New College students in October, 1953, on just what it meant to be a 'Fresher' starting off as a Member of New College and a Member of the University of Oxford (Smith, 1963).

Smith speaks: of undergraduate study as developing 'patience and perseverance and the determination to understand the nature of a problem and the conditions necessary for its solution'; of 'integrity of mind and an unswerving regard for the truth'; of 'steadiness of mind'; of 'a quiet and secure temper of mind'; of 'membership of a society [the college] united in a common purpose'; and of 'a long tradition with its visible embodiment everywhere in the buildings of your College'. His 1953 words are difficult to improve upon half a century later, just as are Cardinal Newman's from a century before Smith. Newman's *The Idea of a University* (1852) has been described by a major scholar of university education as 'unquestionably the single most important treatise in the English language on the nature and meaning of higher education' (Rothblatt, 1997, p 287). Newman defined the values of a Liberal Education: 'The process of training, by which the intellect, instead of being formed or sacrificed to some particular or accidental purpose, some specific trade or profession, or study or science, is disciplined for its own sake, for the perception of its own proper object, and for its own highest culture, is called Liberal Education... And to set forth the right standard, and to train according to it, and to help forward all students towards it according to their various capacities, this I conceive to be the business of a University... Liberal Education makes not the Christian, not the Catholic, but the gentleman. It is well to be a gentleman, it is well to have a cultivated intellect, a delicate taste, a candid, equitable, dispassionate mind, a noble and courteous bearing on the conduct of life – these are the connatural qualities of a large knowledge; they are the objects of a University...' (For more on Newman see earlier in this Chapter and also the Preface to the Chinese translation of this text, reproduced in English at the end of this book.)

This book is for dipping into, now and in the future after some experience of the tutorial system in action: it is certainly not for reading through all in one session. Perhaps first you should read only the essay on or nearest to your own subject. Perhaps you should begin with the Chapter on the theory of student learning (Chapter 11). Or perhaps you could start with the essay from a recent survivor of Oxford's tutorials (Chapter 12). Or maybe with Chapter 13 on students' experiences of the Oxford Tutorial: although you could be a little alarmed at the statement of one of Dr Clark's interviewees that 'the best tutorials are like *Newsnight* with the tutor as

Paxman'. (Paxman as Socrates? – see Chapter 6 on the use of the Socratic Method in tutorial teaching.) You are now embarking on *higher* education (as defined and discussed earlier in this Chapter, and also in Chapters 2 and 11); you are beginning to take much greater control of your learning; so *you* decide where to start with what follows. If the liberal education you receive at Oxford is successful the University and colleges achieve their joint objective, and one shared by all great universities as neatly summed up by a former President of Harvard University: 'Our job is to educate free, independent, and vigorous minds capable of analysing events, of exercising judgement, of distinguishing facts from propaganda and truth from half-truths and lies, and – in the most creative of these at least – of apprehending further reaches of truth…' (Nathan M. Pusey, *The Age of the Scholar*, 1963). And you will then have experienced an intellectual break-through in your learning, as graphically explained by a professor at an English civic university over half-a-century ago: '… it is a great day when he [the undergraduate] throws off the shackles of the text-book, develops a limited trust in his own judgement and conceives a great longing for the time to come when he can trust it more…'; this is 'university education' as opposed to mere 'university instruction' and kicks in once the student gets beyond seeing university as 'a superior kind of school', gets beyond being academically 'spoon-fed', and gets beyond 'a pathetic [and 'misplaced] confidence in the printed word' (Bruce Truscot, *Red Brick University*, 1943). It is hoped that this little book will help you with that intellectual and academic process. Best Wishes for a challenging, stimulating and enjoyable undergraduate career!

Conclusion: delivering a 'liberal education' by adequately engaging the 'higher education' student in continuous 'academic discourse' so as to maximise 'critical-thinking'...

What do students want? Feedback! Attention! A response! Discussion!

UK National Student (Satisfaction) Survey (NSS at www.thestudentsurvey.com): students want 'feedback', contact with faculty (but not necessarily more by way of teaching via lectures).

HEPI Report No. 33 (2007) on 'The Academic Experience of Students in English Universities' (at www.hepi.ac.uk): students work longer per week when there is such 'feedback' and contact (note the commentary by Professor Gibbs on the HEPI Report, and the likely link between assessment methods and student enthusiasm and engagement).

Why do students want it? Such 'feedback' is perhaps *the* most influential while also most neglected aspect of HE teaching practice, but it is labour-intensive and hence expensive (especially if done face-to-face rather than merely by way of a written commentary on a piece of assessed work when returned along with the formal mark). And it must be stressed that 'feedback' is not just about increasing 'contact' hours within a course/module, although 'contact' between student and academic has indeed declined woefully as seminar sizes have at least doubled in recent decades: in fact, HEPI Report No. 36 (2008) comments that UK HE degree courses risk being perceived as 'study light'! Indeed, the Vice-Chancellor of one major UK university has publicly stated: '... this downward trend in teaching hours has occurred over the past 20 years in almost all British universities. The simple fact is that decades of diminishing per capital investment in undergraduate learning in the UK [the amount spent per year on an undergraduate's education – 'the Unit of Resource' – has almost halved since the early-1980s] is having the slow, inevitable consequences for the quality of student learning that were bound to develop...' (Professor Gilbert, Manchester University, *Times Higher* 24/4/08). Hence the University of Manchester is now 'determined to re-personalise the student learning experience, and provide all students with the kind of one-to-one learning that has become increasingly notable by its absence'. Similarly, the University of Lancaster has recently pledged to provide at least 10 contact hours per teaching week for its undergraduates, and other HEIs (for example, the University of Sussex in response to well-publicised complaints from its Union of Students; and at LSE, where teaching is to receive greater resources and its status to be brought closer to that of research) are also reviewing the delivery of undergraduate education... which is just as well in the political context of the 2009/10 parliamentary review of the too-low tuition fees cap of £3000 per annum for 'home' undergraduates, since the much-needed and much hoped-for increase (if it happens) will, rightly, leave students (and their parents) demanding better evidence of value-for-money!

What, as a minimum, should students get? (Recognising that the gold-standard of the Oxford Tutorial is too expensive a teaching process for most universities.) Here is a twenty-first century 'Student Charter' covering the crucial aspect of 'the student experience' in terms of 'teaching and learning' (NB for the sciences and for technology subjects adjust for laboratory practicals, field trips, problem classes)...

- teaching in Year 1 and Year 2 to take place also in Term 3 and not just in Term 1 and in Term 2 as, shamefully, at some HEIs
- seminars of 1:12 (or fewer)
- each student to 'prepare and present' in such seminars once per Term/Semester/Module/Unit
- such seminars to be led by 'full' faculty at least 75% of the time (*ie* limited use of 'adjunct', 'part-time', 'casual' faculty)
- for each item of formally-assessed summative course-work, there should be two items of informal 'academic discourse' formative written-work as 'practice'
- each item of such written-work (formal or informal, assessed or practice) to be the subject of ¼hr, 1:1, oral, face-to-face 'feedback' from the Seminar Leader/Course Assessor-Marker
- all students to have an Academic Tutor with whom they meet (1:1) for ½ hr each Term/Semester to discuss overall progress, study skills, option choices.

So, what is higher *education?* Hence the inputs/outputs/black-box process equation might be:

higher education if really to be higher
= liberal education as a teaching and learning process
= instilling the life-long skill of critical-thinking via reflective-learning and deep-learning that, in turn, nurture radical-thinking and an innovative mind
= ensuring adequate student engagement in the academic discourse
= careful provision of staff: student contact/feedback and using formative assessment...

This is the Oxford Tutorial as a pedagogical process, as Liberal Education. It is stressed that this concept of Liberal Education as a process that develops critical-thinking, reflective-learning or deep-learning is a concept equally applicable to any degree subject or academic discipline offered by a university under the label 'higher education': Liberal Education is not just about the humanities and social studies! And it is also stressed, yet again (!), that there is nothing 'higher' about being a student in higher education unless this intellectual process is taking place, although, worryingly, 'there is now a strong perception that university education is a system of simple quali-fication – like passing the driving test' ('Annual Report, 2007, of the Office of the Independent Adjudicator for Higher Education: Resolving Student Complaints' at www.oiahe.org.uk). The retiring Adjudicator (Baroness Ruth Deech) has made the telling analogy that higher education is not about the student passively receiving a service (teaching) in return for the payment of tuition fees; it is closer to gym membership where the infrastructure and advice is provided but, annoyingly, considerable personal effort is needed if the desired results are to be achieved! (See Chapter 14, 'The Student as Consumer?', in Farrington & Palfreyman (2006) for further discussion). In effect, the Oxford Tutorial is a teaching and learning method that builds on the very simple, but also very important idea that one of the most effective ways to learn about something is to write about it: to gather in material (that, in isolation, would not readily register in the mind) and then to digest it in the context of answering a question, to synthesise it, to play with it, to think hard about it, and to use it in order to answer that essay question – and, crucially, next to discuss its use in this way when attending the tutorial and presenting the essay. Hence the teaching material itself is absorbed more deeply, and also the whole process steadily develops the individual's learning skills and technique.

What higher *education is not!* Indeed, in effect, the call in this book is for the 're-enchantment' of 'the McUniversity' – see Hayes & Wynyard (2006) and, more widely, Ritzer (2008 & 2005) for the concept of the 'McDonaldization' of society and of HE within society; also Furedi (forthcoming). (Note, however, that McDonaldization is not always a bad thing: one might welcome 'McRail' or 'McBus' if it meant hyper-efficient and predictable public transport!) The point is that the over-emphasis on economic efficiency, predictable outcomes, and managerial control risks damping-down, or even killing-off, research radicalness, creativity, innovation, and exciting ideas that are the essence of higher education, while also dumbing-down the challenge of the liberal education teaching and learning process that again is crucial to the real university. This is a problem that, sadly, can only get worse at the ludicrous Bologna Process increasingly impacts on UK HE, and, terrifyingly, if BP 'soft-law' gets incorporated into the potential 'hard-law' of EU directives for implementation by the ever-burgeoning Brussels bureaucracy ('the McBolognarisation of HE'!). To repeat what was stressed in the first section of this Chapter: true higher education is not tertiary education, it is not schooling for adults, it is not a public service like Council waste-collection or State schools, it is not all about skills and competencies, it is not about social engineering, it is not about directly contributing to the growth of the Economy or the health of Society, it is not about a facile rhetoric of 'engagement' with some latest silly whim or obsession of a politician or think-tank, it is not elitist, it is not about feeding employers with what they may short-sightedly see as fit-for-purpose graduates, it is not vocational training, it is not about making students into contented customers, and it is not some sort of touchy-feely therapeutic process where students are painlessly graduated without ever leaving their intellectual comfort zones.

And what is 'critical-thinking', 'reflective-learning' or 'deep-learning'? It is not possible to provide convenient definitions of these concepts; like education itself they imply and involve a life-long, open-ended journey (as indeed hinted at in the quote from Truscot a few pages back). There is, however, plenty of material at the Foundation for Critical Thinking (www.criticalthinking.org) and many texts available in Blackwells and other good bookshops as 'study guides' for the undergraduate, but here is a neat description of 'the intellectually engaged student' (from the Foundation's literature): such a student…

- takes ownership of content through actively thinking it through
- values questions more than answers
- seeks understanding over rote memorization
- assesses thinking for its clarity, accuracy, precision, relevance, depth, breadth, logic, and significance
- seeks to identify key structural components in thinking
- reads, writes, listens, and speaks critically
- questions the thinking of others and expects his or her thinking to be questioned by others
- thinks for himself/herself while respecting and empathically entering the point of view of others
- locates ultimate intellectual authority in evidence and reasoning.

Again, a student charter? This call for extra written work that is not formally marked 'for-the-transcript', and for oral feedback on it, is about the student being given the teaching and learning space and the intellectual freedom (safely outside of the rigidity of the formal assessment process with its predicted learning-outcomes and its predetermined mark-scheme) so as to be able to assess and develop novel interpretations, to display innovative and radical thinking, to explore and to play with ideas. And, above all, preferably even to enjoy participating in this academic discourse within higher education as a re-enchanted process of liberal education. This is a manifesto for the delivery of better higher education that, hopefully, also chimes with the emerging concept of the student as a consumer seeking value-for-money in the context of increasing tuition fees. It is a student charter for the twenty-first century designed to correct the drift towards the 'McUniversity' where 'students may feel like little more than objects into which knowledge is poured as they move along an information-providing and degree-granting educational assembly line' (Ritzer, 2008). Thus, perhaps HE can avoid the fate of Victorian education portrayed by Dickens in 'Hard Times' (1854) where Mr Gradgrind declares of the children ('the little pitchers') in his 'model school' that they must be 'filled so full of facts' by the new teacher, Mr M'Choakumchild: 'Now, what I want is, Facts. Teach these boys and girls nothing but Facts… Stick to Facts, Sir! … In this life, we want nothing but Facts, Sir; nothing but Facts!'

FURTHER READING

See also the texts on Liberal Education cited alongside the relevant quotation/author in the section of this Chapter on *What is 'Liberal Education'?*

Allison, W. (1998) 'Science Teaching and the Tutorial', *Oxford Magazine*, No. 156, 3-4.

Ashwin, P. (2005) 'Variation in students' experiences of the Oxford tutorial', *Higher Education* 50, 631-644.

Ashwin, P. (2006) 'Variation in academics' accounts of tutorials', *Studies in Higher Education* 31 (6), 651-665.

Barr, N. (2001) *The Welfare State as Piggy Bank: Information, Risk, Uncertainty, and the Role of the State.* Oxford: OUP.

Brabazon, T. (2007) *The University of Google: education in the (post) information age.* Aldershot, UK: Ashgate.

Brock, M.G. & Curthoys, M.C. (2000) *The History of the University of Oxford: Volume VII, Nineteenth Century Oxford, Part 2.* Oxford: OUP.

Cartwright, J. (2008) *This Secret Garden: Oxford Revisited.* London: Bloomsbury.

Cobban, A.B. (1988) *The Medieval English Universities: Oxford and Cambridge to 1500.* Aldershot: Scolar Press.

Cobban, A.B. (1999) *English university life in the Middle Ages.* London: UCL Press.

Curzon, Lord (1909) *Principles and Methods of University Reform.* Oxford: OUP.

Duke, A. (1996) *Importing Oxbridge: English Residential Colleges and American Universities.* New Haven, CT: Yale University Press

Engel, A. (1993) *From Clergyman to Don: The Rise of the Academic Profession in Nineteenth-Century Oxford.* Oxford: Clarendon Press.

Evans, M. (2004) *Killing Thinking: the death of the universities.* London: Continuum.

Farrington, D. & Palfreyman, D. (2006) *The Law of Higher Education.* Oxford: Oxford University Press.

Franks Commission (1966) *Commission of Inquiry: Report.* Oxford: Clarendon Press.

Furedi, F. (forthcoming) *The End of Education.*

Harrison, B. (1994) *The History of the University of Oxford: Volume VIII, The Twentieth Century.* Oxford: OUP.

Hayes, D. & Wynyard (2006) *The McDonaldization of Higher Education.* Westport, CT: Bergin & Garvey.

Howard-Johnston, J. (2006) 'In Praise of the Tutorial', *Oxford Magazine*, No. 247, 4.

Kennedy, D. (1997) *Academic Duty.* Cambridge, MA: Harvard University Press.

Lucas, J.R. (1996) 'In Defence of Teaching', *Oxford Magazine*, No. 131, 5.

Lucas, J.R. (1999) 'A Don's Defence', *Journal of the Oxford Society*, Vol. LI, No. 2, 59-64.

Mallinson, C. (1941) 'The Oxford Tutorial', *Southwest Review* 27 (1), 123-134.

Moodie, G. (2008), *From Vocational to Higher Education: An International Perspective.* Maidenhead: Open University Press.

Moore, W.G. (1968) *The Tutorial System and its Future.* Oxford: Pergamon Press.

Naylor, R. (2007) *Whose Degree Is It Anyway? – Why, How and Where Universities are Failing Our Students.* [www.pencil-sharp.com].

Newman, J.H. (1852) *The Idea of a University.*

North Report (1997) *Commission of Inquiry Report.* Oxford: Oxford University Press.

OxCHEPS & The Ulanov Partnership (2004), 'Costing, funding and sustaining higher education: a case study of Oxford University', in *Higher Education Review* 37(1) 3-31 – also at the Papers page of the OxCHEPS website.

Palfreyman, D. (2007), 'Sustaining Oxford as World Class', in H. de Burgh et al (eds), *Can the Prizes Still Glitter? The Future of British Universities in a Changing World* (AGORA; University of Buckingham Press).

Palfreyman, D. (2004) *The Economics of Higher Education: Affordability and Access; Costing, Pricing and Accountability.* Oxford: OxCHEPS. (Also online as Item 10 at the Papers page of the OxCHEPS web-site.)

Panton, J. (2004), 'Challenging Students', in The *RoutledgeFalmer Guide to Key Debates in Education*, D. Hayes (ed), London: RoutledgeFalmer.

Ritzer, G. (2008) *The McDonaldization of Higher Education*. Los Angeles: Pine Forge Press.

Ritzer, G. (2005) *Enchanting a Disenchanted World: Revolutionising the Means of Consumption*. Los Angeles: Pine Forge Press.

Rose, J. & Ziman, J. (1964) *Camford Observed*. London: Victor Gollancz.

Rothblatt, S. (1997) 'An Oxonian "Idea" of a University: J.H. Newman and "Well-Being" ', in M.G. Brock & M.C. Curthoys, *The History of the University of Oxford: Volume VI, Nineteenth Century Oxford, Part 1* (pp 287-305; Oxford: OUP).

Royal Commission (1922) *Royal Commission on Oxford and Cambridge Universities*. London: HMSO.

Ryan, A. (1998) *Liberal Anxieties and Liberal Education*. New York: Hill & Wang.

Ryan, M.B. (2001) *A Collegiate Way of Living: Residential Colleges and a Yale Education*. Newhaven, CT: Yale University.

Siedentop, L. (2000) *Democracy in Europe*. London: Penguin.

Skelton, A. (2007) *International Perspectives on Teaching Excellence in Higher Education*. London: Routledge.

Smith, A.H. (1963) *Selected Essays and Addresses*. Oxford: Blackwell's.

Tapper, T. & Palfreyman, D. (2000) *Oxford and the Decline of the Collegiate Tradition*. London: Woburn Press. (Second edition, forthcoming, Springer).

Trigwell, K. & Ashwin, P. (2003) *Undergraduate Students' Experience of Learning at the University of Oxford*. (online at www.learning.ox.ac.uk).

Warner, D. & Palfreyman, D. (2001) *The State of UK Higher Education: Managing Change and Diversity*. Buckingham: Open University Press. (See especially Chapter 2 on Oxford.)

2. A Liberal Education: and that includes the Sciences!
Alan Ryan, Warden, New College

Discussions of liberal education commonly take off from John Henry Newman's little masterpiece, *The Idea of a University* (1852). A liberal education itself, however, must begin many years before the future undergraduate even contemplates applying for university. My own came in two phases, one beginning very early, the other beginning several years after. One way of suggesting that liberal education is neither very esoteric, nor – as Newman said it was – the process of making a young man into 'a gentleman' is to sketch what it was for a working-class child in North London, immediately after the end of World War II.

My parents left school at thirteen, my mother to become a housemaid in Liverpool and my father to become a boy clerk in London. Both were clever; and both regretted their missed education. My father was particularly conscious of the education he had not had, not because he felt vulnerable to intellectual snobbery or the condescension of colleagues with an expensive and prolonged education, but because he believed that the world contained riches of which he was unaware, and especially that there were innumerable interesting ideas that he had to hunt out while his more privileged contemporaries had had them thrust upon them.

One of my parents' resources was the public library system – among the others were the Operatic Society of what later became the Polytechnic and then the University of North London, together with seats in the amphitheatre at Sadler's Wells. The Holloway Road branch of Islington public library was as important in my education as the Drayton Park primary school where I passed six years from 1945 to 1951. A benign children's librarian did not flinch when I took out armfulls of books twice weekly and returned them after reading them cover to cover; instead, she got me a non-fiction ticket to the adult section of the library, where a colleague talked me through what I might plausibly read at the age of seven and interrogated me gently on what I made of what I consumed.

In what sense was this a liberal education – or the start of one, or the laying of its foundations? In order to answer that question, a diversion is needed. A vice of many, probably most, discussions of education at all levels is their one-sidedness; the tyranny of 'either-or,' bemoaned in many places, is somehow accepted in educational discussions. Is education supposed to be vocational or liberal; do we learn for instrumental reasons or for its own sake; is education intrinsically a process of life-long learning or something we should finish at eighteen; and so generally on. And when we embark on the analysis of one area or other, we find the same fixation on the need to find one answer for all questioners.

Is a liberal education meant to instil a decent humility in the learner as she or he contemplates the 'best that is thought and said in the world,' or should it equip the intrepid traveller with intellectual crampons and ice-axes so that she can climb peaks never before attempted and survey the world from a height never reached before? Is the idea of a liberal education, that is to say, essentially conservative or essentially radical? When it comes to content, we find ourselves equally at the mercy of either-or: Is a liberal education essentially literary and historical, so that we must contrast the liberal and the scientific, or should we aspire to an education in which the student of Proust turns as happily to the mysteries of the solar neutrino for intellectual refreshment as the physicist turns to the novels of Stendahl?

It is clear that what I got was a liberal education – though it was in various ways narrower than it decently could and should have been; and it really started when I was seven years old. It was only one of many possible shapes that a liberal education might take, and in what follows I want to explain what the point of it was for me, in the hope that some of it rings true to some readers' experience, and that what does not will provoke them to think what else might. First, then, to reduce some familiar oppositions.

A liberal education is not of its nature non-vocational. Historically, a liberal education was one suited to persons looking to a career in the liberal professions – the church, law and medicine. But, history aside, a liberal education will give its beneficiaries skills that are useful in almost every walk of life, and increasingly so in the modern world and the so-called knowledge economy. Recent governments have become obsessed with transferable skills; a liberal education provides them under another name, and always has done. The ability to read exactly and absorb information swiftly and in recapturable form; the ability to speak and write coherently and lucidly so that new information or a new step in an argument follows transparently from its predecessor and leads transparently to its successor; the ability to see the implications of numerical data and to elicit them from different presentations – these are what a liberally educated person can do, and what almost any white-collar occupation makes some use of.

Of course, there is a difference between an education's being vocational in the sense of providing the broad capacities for any occupation and its being vocational in the sense of providing the more focused skills required for one particular occupation. To become an accomplished manager in the hotel industry, you need to learn a great deal about the hotel industry in particular, work in hotels in different countries, and work in different parts of a hotel. In so doing, you will learn a good many things that will not migrate easily to other occupations, as well as a number that certainly will. The same thing is true, however, of the particular things you will need to learn if you join the civil service and find yourself organising military procurement, or if you become a doctor specialising in disorders of the urinary tract, or a journalist and discover that working on *The Guardian* is as different as you had thought it might be from working on *The Sun*. There is a contrast, not between a liberal education and an education that improves a student's employability, but between an education that provides a broad-gauge capacity for employment, and training in the particular branch of employment at issue.

I say this with some feeling, since I became a university teacher entirely by accident. To the extent that I thought about future occupations before I found myself employed, I assumed that I would become a lawyer or a journalist. Both offered a high degree of autonomy and a chance to exercise a liking for picking up stray bits of factual information and constructing an argument out of them. I was tempted by the thought of a career in the Foreign Office or the Treasury, but feared having to work long hours, wear a suit and keep a tidy desk. It was not only the relaxed climate of the early 1960s that made me so insouciant about where I should earn my living; it was also the sense that the point of the education I had had was to allow one to lift one's head, look around, and consider which of the world's opportunities was most worth taking.

So, if the contrast between vocational and liberal education can be deflated – leaving unexplored the further contrast between training and education – we can return to **the question of what a liberal education is and why it is worth having**. I start with another autobiographical story. When I was fourteen, the school teacher who taught history to my peers and me asked us what we had done during the vacation; we answered something or other, and one of us politely inquired what *he* had been doing. He said that his parents had been celebrating his father's seventy-fifth birthday, and offered to show us some photographs of the event. As it happened, his father was Russian and Jewish, and a world-famous 'cellist – all of this was more or less unbeknown to us – and his parents lived in Vence in the south of France. So there at the lunch table were Casals and Chagall. Our jaws dropped. We had, I assume, not exactly doubted that Matisse and Picasso were real people, known to other real people as friends, lovers, colleagues, reluctant or cooperative providers of works of art for exhibition and sale; but we had no idea that they were *really* real people. Now we believed it.

So, one thing liberal education is for is to give the student who is getting educated the strongest possible sense that the world is genuinely there to be enjoyed, and that it is not merely possible to look at the astonishing things human beings have done, but to participate in the process of their creation and take ownership of the results. This is what became clear to my fourteen year old self, though in a prefatory and incomplete fashion. 'Ownership,' though it has become a cliché of modern management-speak, has a good pedigree, and a little elaboration on the idea is needed, not least because it will take us to the upshot of this essay – the thought that a liberal education is an education in intellectual freedom.

At first sight, **ownership** is exactly what we do *not* have when we learn to enjoy some part of the almost infinite riches of the mind; ordinarily, what is 'mine' cannot be 'thine,' at least, not without considerable complications about joint or common ownership, and not without taking on board the ways in which what you can do restricts and limits what I can do. If we jointly own a cycle, neither of us can sell it without the other's permission, or, if either of us can, we have to hand over half the proceeds when we do so. Ideas are not like that, and neither is the experience of enjoying music, painting, architecture, or the landscape. Certainly paintings are owned, and bought and sold for enormous sums of money; musical scores are owned and recordings are copyrighted; most of the landscape belongs to someone or other. What does not in that literal and exclusive sense belong to anyone is the point or purpose of these things, that is to say our experience and enjoyment of them.

If the French government owns most of the very few paintings by de la Tour that survive, it does not own their appreciation, nor the pleasure they give, nor an understanding of the impact they have on the spectator. Beethoven's late quartets exist more importantly as manifested in performance after performance than as scores; at one level, all the scores consist of is ink marks on paper, it is the understanding of what those marks mean as instructions to musicians that turns them into the scores of the late quartets and it is the performances that the musicians give that make those instructions important.

All this might suggest – as it has done to innumerable social critics – that we must draw a sharp distinction between those things that *can* and those that *cannot* be owned, with the goods of the mind belonging very firmly to the latter category. This is a point worth making if we want to say that when a corporation buys a Van Gogh and hangs it on the boardroom wall, it has not bought a painting but merely exchanged one cheque for another. The thing on the wall, like the cheque with which it was purchased, simply says 'the owners of this are good for ever so many millions of pounds.' To serve any more elevated purpose, it has to be looked at with appreciative eyes for other purposes. We not say this in any censorious spirit; we may, after all, gaze on our neighbour's Ferrari and wish we had the money to waste on such a toy, and we may gaze on our neighbour's Van Gogh and wish we had the money to hang such a thing on our wall, even if we don't particularly like Van Gogh.

So what sort of 'ownership' is it that we might have of an experience that cannot in the usual sense be owned by anyone? The thought is surely this. What owners of things have is a form of freedom. Negatively, they may use whatever they own in ways other people may not interfere with. I can do things to my house or car that other people may not prevent me doing. I can also give it or sell it to other people; and I can experiment with turning it into something other than the house or car I first acquired.

So with ideas. Many of us spend a lot of time recycling ideas that are only in the thinnest sense our own; they are ideas we have never thought through, never examined for their credibility or coherence, never tried to integrate with the rest of our mental and emotional stock. In relation to them, we are not much more than pieces of blank paper on which someone has scribbled a few thoughts, and off which other people can read those same thoughts. Nothing has happened to those thoughts as they have been passed to us and passed on from us. They are very much not *our* thoughts. There have been some writers – the American pragmatists among them – who have been tempted to say that under these conditions, it is not really true that 'we think' whatever it might be; more exactly, 'thought happens' and it is only when we take some responsibility for the thought that is happening that we can properly say that 'we think.'

This may be an exaggerated way of making the point, but the point is important. **A liberal education is one that aims to take us to the point where we think, or to put it another way, where the ideas we use are really our ideas**. It aims at a sort of **freedom for the mind**. This is the freedom that comes when we have a relation to our ideas that is not fearful or anxious, not coloured by the wish to think what it is respectable to think, nor what we think our teachers would wish us to think or our examiners would wish us to write down. It is what we have when we can put ourselves in the shoes of the people who are vastly cleverer or more imaginative or insightful or more deft than ourselves, and then can work our way through their achievements for ourselves.

We may, when we have done this, want to go on and do more of it for ourselves – but we may not. There is a temptation to think that mastering a subject must then lead on to what is usually described as 'research,' and for preference research at the 'cutting edge.' But it need not; and indeed, for almost all of us in almost every field of inquiry or creation, it simply cannot. What liberal education fosters is not a respect for research so much as a **respect for scholarship**; and in doing so, it illuminates what is futile in most discussions of the relationship between teaching and research. The defence of the usefulness of cutting edge research to everyday undergraduate teaching is at best implausible and often duplicitous. *Some* cutting edge researchers are exceedingly good at conveying the excitement of novel discoveries to undergraduate audiences; most would rather be in the laboratory or in the field making the discoveries. The thought that it is impossible to be a good teacher without engaging in cutting edge research is as utterly implausible as the thought that all cutting edge researchers would like to teach.

What is not implausible is the thought that good scholarship is needed for good teaching. That, after all, is no more than the thought that if we are to transmit a mastery of something, we need to have acquired at least enough dexterity of our own to show someone else the direction in which they can acquire a mastery greater than our own. Consider the good tennis coach and the great tennis player; the player can do what the coach cannot do – but the coach knows why it matters to do it and what it is like to do it well. Good teaching conveys a respect for and an enjoyment of – to recur to Matthew Arnold – the best that is thought and said in the world. It does not teach cutting edge research techniques.

But this is where we can home in on what it is that liberal education achieves. It provides the intellectual freedom that those who attain it would not wish to be without. It is consistent with the deepest respect for previous achievement – indeed, it is hard to see how one could be seriously engaged in thinking at all without feeling something very like reverence for the insight, imagination, perseverance, and sheer strenuousness of the thinking of one's predecessors. To hanker after mastering a subject is hard to imagine without imagining also the idea of an intellectual master – in an ungendered sense of that term – for whom one feels genuine respect.

This is why Matthew Arnold was so wrong to suppose that science cannot play a part in liberal education. Leaving aside the fact that so many of the greatest scientists seem to be driven by something akin to a sense of the poetry of the world – thus closing the gap between literature and art that Arnold opened up – one should take seriously is the less often uttered thought that literature aims to show us the world in all its intricacy just as science does. A respect for meticulous observation and imaginative understanding is not fostered only by one discipline; it is common to all serious investigation of both the world and ourselves. Certainly, there is an emphasis in science conceived as an element of a liberal education that is not on all fours with research training; but then the emphasis in the study of English literature as an element in a liberal education is not on all fours with the concerns of the research student poring over watermarks.

But that, after all, is consistent with acknowledging some familiar truths about freedom. To attain it may require a great deal of self-discipline; to be the masters of our own intellectual lives we have to be able to think consecutively and cogently, and that takes time, patience, and application. To think freely, and to be in command of our thinking and understanding is an accomplishment that does not come particularly easily; as Mill observed, human beings are so much creatures of habit that habitual responses are not only second nature, they are usually mistaken for first nature. To be able really to direct our attention and understanding to fruitful targets and to get from experience the full value it has to offer is from the – mildly self-centred perspective proper to a discussion of what liberal education does for those who get it – perhaps as good a summary of the point of liberal education as we here need.

3. Teaching Law, Learning Law: Growing Up Intellectually
Peter Mirfield, Fellow in Law, Jesus College

In Chapter 1 the Editor of this work refers to "consumers" and "producers". Many of the contributors will have been both, myself included. I suspect that I am not the only one for whom what one found so valuable as consumer, one proposes to try to promote as producer.

It was my "luck" to be asked to read out my essay at the very first tutorial any of the first-year lawyers at my old college had ever attended. First, be it noted – and this is very much part of the tradition – it took place at another college. The subject-matter was, as I recall, something to do with slavery in Roman Law. I had done all the reading, that is, at least my eyes had followed the words, and I did have "good notes". But, in order to write the essay, I gathered together chunks from the various writings, glued them together in some sort of order. It looked a very neat product, and I went contentedly to sleep.

Contentment disappeared when I got the call to read. My recollection is that I managed to get four words out before my interlocutor intervened, although, on reflection, I think it may have been ten or twelve. I am sure that his words were, 'What do you mean by that?'. The truth was that I did not mean anything by it – the point came from someone far more expert than I could ever be. Yet, something told me that that was not the appropriate response. So, I suppose I mumbled something inconsequential. Escape was not as easy as that. Forty-five or fifty minutes later, I was allowed respite, having proceeded, I think, to the end of the second paragraph.

This was no Pauline conversion. I was embarrassed, certainly. I probably told my colleagues, as they commiserated with me, that the man who had made me suffer was a sadistic swine. Indeed, I cannot have learned much about Roman Law, even by two terms later, when I managed a gamma plus in Law Moderations. However, the lesson did sink in, and especially as it was reinforced by all the other tutors that I faced. He was neither sadistic, nor a swine. He simply wanted me to know that I was now at a place where I was in charge of my studies, where I was responsible for them, and where it was irrelevant that the texts were written by people more expert than I could ever be. In short, I was expected to grow up intellectually.

My own tutor never treated me otherwise than as his equal. We both recognized that I knew far less than did he, but that was for me to cure. When I failed to come up to the mark of understanding, or had worked insufficiently hard, or thought too little, he was disappointed, not angry. When I did get an inkling of what a topic might really be about, he probably told me that I seemed to have sorted it out. By the end of three years, I think that I almost had.

In other words, the subject-matter being studied is fundamentally unimportant. How it is studied is what matters. That truth is not described by either party, but simply becomes understood as the thread that binds tutor to student.

Now, as one of the producers, I suppose that I hope I may pay back something of what I took out. Like all good things, the tutorial is not an unallayed good. I have given many a poor tutorial, and I have had a few lousy tutorial students. No less, I am sure, than many others, I have wondered why I was seeking to explain some point of difficulty for a sixth time to a puzzled pair of undergraduates. Would it not have been better to deliver a mini-lecture to the lot of them, dealing with that point? Perhaps, but, for each of them, it was the first time they had asked the question and the first time it had been answered. And, at least if I was in good form and had my eye in, it would be the undergraduate that eventually answered the question for himself or herself (possibly without appreciating it).

Then, of course, there are the silent ones. I distinctly recall soon after becoming a Fellow, taking a young woman who left her tutorial partner to make all the going. He had the decency to fill the silences for her when I addressed the question directly at her. So I decided to take her on her own. Ready for the task, I swore to myself that I would not let her of the hook. The question was put, and the silence began. It seemed to go on forever. Initially, I kept my nerve, but she was the stronger party, and I ended up the filling the void. Afterwards, I castigated myself for my own weakness, but, I have come to think, with the passage of time, that she was the real loser. Bluntly, there are some who are unsuited to the tutorial idea, and there is nothing that can be done about it. It is better to look at the other side. The undergraduate gets to know the tutor. If shy, that can gradually stop getting in the way, and I really remember occasions when, after a halting start, such a person began to engage in the process of discovery, perhaps without even realising it.

What about the tutor? The main problems are, I suspect, not boredom (although this does, of course, impinge at times), but expertise and self-esteem. I am afraid that many tutors (although, I am confident, not the other contributors to this collection) get a kick out of having understood something, so much so that they cannot bear not to lay it before their captive audience. We may even sound good as we do it, and the brightest students, in particular, will be suitably impressed. Yet, we are doing it for ourselves, not asking them to do it for themselves. At least with the subject that bats, say, fourth in a descending order of expertise, I will have that ordinary (and proper) fear that I may have missed the point somewhere. (That is not to say that I will not miss a point in my own area of expertise, just that I will not fear it.) I may, like my pupils, have boned up the latest cases only the night before, so that we enter together on a voyage of discovery. Some of them will think that I really should know the stuff, if I am to teach it to them. The better ones will work out that expertise is fragile, disappearing like the morning mist. What is left is method, and experience of exposing material across a whole range of topics to that method. Of course, I too could be better-organised and work harder, but there are other calls on my time, no less than on theirs.

There is a downside of the tutorial essay that one ought always to have in mind. I am very much in favour of something having to be written for each tutorial. Nothing exposes one's own lack of understanding of a topic. Therefore, it is the process of planning and writing the essay that is the purpose of the exercise. Yet, if the student ends up with, say, eight long essays on the most important topics in the Law of Contract, there is a tendency for those essays to become *the* Law of Contract. Examiners have plenty of experience of the candidate who forces his or her old essay into the question on the paper that it most nearly fits. It is an irony that a method of teaching designed to open up argument sometimes ends up with a text that closes off argument. Against that, in the final term, set aside for revision and including revision tutorials, I reckon that I can tell which students are going to get the best degrees. They are the ones who are still thinking. In Law, perhaps unlike (at least to the same degree) any other subject, we are always a prey to the latest groundbreaking new material, say a case from our highest court, the House of Lords. Many students think that the new material, barely understood, will push out the old material, reasonably well understood, from the brain, wreaking confusion everywhere. The better ones, and especially the best ones, know that no argument in law, any less than in, say, philosophy, is ever concluded, but is merely adjourned. New cases may bring in fresh ideas or insights; they certainly provide us with a new way of looking at the old material. I remember another of my tutors here telling me that the hugely important tort case, Hedley Byrne v Heller, was reported in "The Times" on the very day he took that paper in Finals. He told us how awful it had been, but I did not really believe him.

There will be some discussion, I am sure, in this volume about how the "tutorial system" can and may adapt to a world in which there is more pressure upon academics than ever before to produce research. I will put to one side the example of a college tutor who described tutorial teaching as getting in the way of his work, but who probably needed a gentle reminder from the Bursar of his college that he is paid to do that which gets in the way. My attention is upon those who are thoroughly conscientious, but who find the present tutorial load too much. Many are using different teaching methods and styles, the effect of which is to reduce the number of hours that they teach. Though I would rather we had three tutors each to teach eight hours of tutorials, if that were the proper choice for pedagogical purposes, than two meant to teach twelve but actually teaching eight (to reduce load), money means that I cannot, at present at least, have what I want. But, even then, something of great value still remains. The tutor is responsible for the student's academic studies. He or she arranges the teaching, and oversees their progress as a whole. The result is, or certainly should be, that individuals do not fall down cracks. Failures and weaknesses are noticed early and can be addressed. Successes too do not escape our attention. This is not at all to say that my colleagues in other universities are less attentive to students than we are here in Oxford. Rather, because we have a range of subjects in our Oxford colleges as mini-universities and because we admit our students, the commitment is inevitably closer and more pressing.

I think that I may have been expected to say a little more about the tutorial from a lawyer's point of view. That I have not is, I believe, more a reflection of a viable inter-pretation of the task set by the Editor, rather than a failure to perform that task properly!

4. Modern Linguists as Multi-taskers

Roger Pearson, Fellow in French, Queen's College

Modern Linguists at Oxford are multi-taskers, and the flexibility of the tutorial system offers us many advantages. Language itself, both English and foreign, is at the heart of what we do, whether it be speaking or writing, listening or reading. The way we do it varies from language to language and college to college, but common to all students of Modern Languages is the opportunity to be taught in small groups and to receive individual attention – especially when sometimes you'd rather not!

In the Preliminary Examination, taken at the end of the first year, the emphasis is mainly but not exclusively on the written word, and students are required, for example, to be able to translate into and out of their target language, or to complete a set of grammatical exercises with accuracy, or to write in the target language in response to a piece of contemporary prose. In the 'larger' languages, such as French and German, language teaching generally takes place in colleges in classes of up to six or seven students: work will be set and marked by the tutor, and the class will be devoted to discussing the questions and problems raised by the work set. Some larger, University-based classes are also arranged for supplementary grammar lessons. In other languages, teaching tends to be organised on a University-wide basis, but the classes are small and the attention no less individual. Though this first-year exam has no oral element, you will nevertheless at most colleges find yourself having classes with a native speaker (again in very small groups) and being able to practise your speaking and listening.

The study of a language not only means learning to use that language oneself but also seeing how others use it, particularly those who are good at this! Hence Modern Linguists at Oxford also learn how to analyse literary texts and how to understand them within the historical and cultural context in which these examples of linguistic art were written. Here the tutorial has a vital role to play. While there are many lecture courses on the writers and works concerned, providing useful background material and offering analysis of the principal thematic and stylistic issues, the main focus of a student's efforts will be a weekly tutorial on a given subject. You will be given a commentary to write or an essay topic to discuss, together with some suggested books or articles to help you. Your work is then assessed by your tutor and the subject itself discussed further in small groups (generally of two or three students only). This may be supplemented by seminar or class discussion in groups of five or six, for which no written work is required but enthusiastic participation is nevertheless a prerequisite!

When you find yourself in a tutorial, face to face with your tutor and accompanied perhaps by only one or two other students, then you will begin to realize the full value of the tutorial system. 'No hiding place' is how some tutors like to describe it, and that goes as much for the tutor as the student. You will not be able to hide at the back and conceal your ignorance; but the tutor, too, is there to be asked – and questioned! The important thing to get straight is that the tutorial is part of an ongoing process of mental development over several years: it's not a mini-inquisition to be endured with the minimum of damage to ego and reputation. From the tutor's point of view the great advantage of the tutorial is that s/he can see immediately how far a student has got with a particular topic and then take them on from there, supplying 'leads' to further enquiry and raising questions which will make the student want to rush off and read and think some more (we hope). From the student's point of view, once you've learnt to trust your tutor and discovered that mistakes or lack of knowledge are not going to meet with some terrible punishment, the tutorial offers a tremendous opportunity to be honest about what you have and haven't mastered yet or what you just can't get your head round at all. And it offers the opportunity to be enthused. In a way the ideal tutorial is one in which you go in thinking you've got the topic sorted and come out realising how much more interesting it actually is – and how much work, alas, you still have to do.

In the second and final years of your course, the options multiply and the tutorial system once again offers invaluable flexibility. You will continue to have language classes in which you learn principally to translate into and out of the target language, and to write essays in it; and you will now receive help from native speakers in preparing for the Oral Examination which is an important element in the Final Examinations. The Year Abroad, and as many visits abroad as possible in the Vacations, are obviously important opportunities to complement this tuition with real live talking, but these small oral classes offer a beneficial setting in which to take the linguistic plunge among friends!

The study of literature and culture widens and deepens, and you will find yourself meeting your tutor in your weekly tutorial with usually only one other student present and sometimes none. Alone at last! Now you don't even have to worry what other students think of you, and you can really show your ignorance – or ask that challenging question which might have sounded like you were showing off. At this stage you may be studying anything from a medieval epic to a novel on the Women's Writing course that was published only last year. But you might also be studying the history of your language – how Old French became Middle French became Modern French – or the nature of language itself and how it 'works' (i.e. Linguistics) or European cinema or literary theory (what *is* a post-structuralist?). In each case you will be involved in some combination of tutorial, class and/or seminar where the numbers are small and the degree of tutor-contact high.

By this time also you will have gradually accumulated a certain familiarity with the history, society, and culture of the country whose language you are studying, and you may want to take this further. Tutors are themselves specialists in particular areas of research, and between them they cover a very wide range of periods and topics. As your own interests gradually harden in one direction or another, you will want to go deeper into some areas. Here again the collegiate tutorial system can be turned to advantage as a tutor at one college can ask a tutor at another to give you tutorials on a subject where this other tutor may well be the leading expert in the field. Rather than being overawed, most students find this kind of situation exciting and challenging. Now you can 'see' the leading edge of the subject and you can pit your own wits against the difficulties, guided by someone whose judgement you can trust and who will know which intellectual steps need to be taken next. And for the tutor this is the best kind of tutorial: where he or she, for all that they may have written the definitive book on the subject, has to defend their position – listening to queries, objections, alternative views, and constantly checking these against their own interpretation of the subject.

And this is why tutors like being tutors. Because however familiar the topic – whether or not they are world experts on it – each student comes to it afresh and thereby renews it in the mind of the tutor. Even the most orthodox essay on Proust will spark off new ideas because the tutor will be busy thinking: well, I've heard all this before but is it really fair to say that the key to Proustian fulfilment is a biscuit and a cup of tea? And, of course, Oxford students are usually more enterprising than that: not geniuses necessarily, or uniformly breathtaking in their insights, but people with energetic and enquiring minds who have a genuine curiosity about things and a very healthy scepticism about pat answers. Which is what keeps us ivy-clad academics on our toes. Which is one of the reasons we admit you in the first place.

5. Evolution in Biology Tutoring?

Richard Dawkins, Charles Simonyi Professor of the Public Understanding of Science, University of Oxford, and Professorial Fellow, New College

The article reproduced below was first published in 1994 under the deliberately graceless title 'Tutorial-Driven', in *The Oxford Magazine[1]*, a semi-official house magazine published fortnightly during Term and read by the University's teaching and research community. It was reprinted two years later in *Oxford Today[2]*, the nearest approach Oxford has to an 'alumni magazine', under the title 'The Way we Teach.' My tone was unabashedly nostalgic and my intention was to resist, perhaps Canute-like, an advancing tide which I thought inimical to scholarship. To an extent, the trends that I was then resisting have continued. Tutorials in Biological Sciences are now more closely synchronised than ever to particular lectures, and undergraduates increasingly demand that their tutorials should prepare them for particular examinations. These demands are met because, to a perhaps surprising extent, the University cares about undergraduate opinion. I quote from my biological colleague Philip Stewart's published response[3] to my original article:

"How wonderful it would be if all Oxford students could have tutorials like those described by Richard Dawkins (*Oxford Magazine*, No. 112)! Perhaps there was a time, not so long ago, when it did happen . . . From listening to today's undergraduates, I get the impression that they live in a quite different world. They expect each tutor to have half a dozen standard topics, each with its standard reading list, and they count on being able to write most of their Finals answers by regurgitating material from their tutorial essays."

If this is true I regret it, for reasons that may be surmised from my 1994 article. But, even so, I continue to think the Oxford Tutorial is better than any alternative on offer. The virtues of individual attention are still there in full. A young relative of mine has recently graduated in Biological Science from another prestigious university. She loved her time there, and enjoyed lectures by excellent scientists. But one problem emerged at the end, which would have been inconceivable at Oxford (or Cambridge). When she came to seek a job and needed testimonials from her teachers, it proved almost impossible to find a quorum who had the faintest idea who she was. At Oxford she could have called upon half a dozen tutors, all of whom would have been on Christian name terms with her (both ways) and all of whom would have been intimately familiar with her work and her strengths. The Oxford Tutorial today may fall a little short of my rose-tinted recollections, but it is still greatly superior to the so-called 'tutorial' (actually usually a seminar or class) in any other university except Cambridge.

And so it should be, one might say, given the cost of the true one-to-one tutorial. When my article was reprinted in *Oxford Today*, it was followed up in a subsequent issue by a thorough analysis of the modern tutorial system by Graham Topping[4]. Topping took account of readers' letters in response to my article, many of which were even more nostalgic than my original, but he also looked at the economics of

[1] No. 112, Eighth week, Michaelmas Term 1994, pp 13-14.
[2] Volume 8, No 3, Trinity Term 1996, pp 4-5.
[3] Oxford Magazine, No. 113, Nought Week, Hilary Term, 1995.

the system. The cost is so great that it cannot be met from income. The tutorial system is a luxury, subsidised by eating into endowment capital. This is no doubt wonderful for today's undergraduates who enjoy the benefits, but it is presumably at the expense of future cohorts. The one-to-one tutorial may be unsustainable in the long-term unless changes are made (see also the discussion in Chapter 1 on the economics of undergraduate teaching).

The obvious response to the economic imperative is to move towards tutoring in pairs, in groups of three, or in groups so large as to belie the name tutorial. This would not be my way. I'd stick with the one-to-one tradition but try to find ways to make it economically viable. I'd do it by reducing the age and qualifications – and cost – of the typical tutor. I would introduce something like the American 'teaching assistant', but acting as tutor rather than just laboratory demonstrator. My 'Tutor Assistants' or 'Junior Tutors' would be graduate students, teaching undergraduates only a few years younger than themselves. They would not be paid much, because the experience of teaching would properly be regarded as an important part of their own education. The Oxford tradition of the one-to-one tutorial with a weekly essay based on readings from original research literature would be maintained. Like American TAs, Junior Tutors would be apprenticed to a more experienced 'Master', who would retain supervisory responsibility for a course of tutorials. In a typical term, an undergraduate could expect, say, two tutorials with a Master and six with Juniors. Perhaps less wise and less knowledgeable than their Master, Junior Tutors would have the enthusiasm of youth, the keenness of novelty, and the empathy which comes from having recently been undergraduates themselves (see Chapter 12).

Although my 1994 article name-dropped tutors who were world-class masters, I really believe there was no need for them to have been that. I still think the Oxford one-to-one tutorial was the making of my entire career. But if I am honest, I think this might have been so even if my tutors had known very little more than I did myself. The important thing was the knowledge that my essay, when I eventually completed it, would be the object of one hour's undivided and serious attention from somebody qualified to judge it and discuss its topic with me at least as an equal. The educational value comes not from listening to what the tutor has to say (as if a tutorial were a private lecture), but from preparing to write essays, from writing them, and from arguing about them in an unrushed session afterwards.

It is the feeling that one's essay will be valued and discussed for a whole hour that makes the writing seem worthwhile. It gives the undergraduate an inkling of how it might feel to be the world authority on a subject. If anything, this valuable educational experience might come better with a Junior Tutor than with a senior scholar who really *is* the world authority and whose prestige and reputation might seem to quell debate. The important thing to retain from Oxford's unique tradition is the whole hour of a tutor's attention, with nobody else present. Not only should Oxford and Cambridge find ways of making the system economically sustainable, but also the model could with advantage be exported to other universities.

⁴ Volume 9, No 3, Trinity Term 1997, ''The Cost of Quality'.

My 1994 article follows…

Tutorial-Driven

We in the biological faculty have been meeting to indulge in one of those satisfying orgies of communal breast-beating that afflict conscientious teachers from time to time. What are we doing wrong? How can we improve the way we teach and the way we examine? Certain other universities are said to do X; surely powerful evidence that X must be a good thing to do. The present examination system unfairly discriminates against students with a short attention span. Shouldn't we be doing continuous assessment like they do at Chipping Ongar? Could we make lecture attendance compulsory like they do at Herne Bay? What do the undergraduates think? (What do the individual undergraduate representatives on the committee think?) How about a clocking-in machine for practical classes? At Crichel Down they have 'tutorials' 20-strong, whereas we have a measly one student per tutorial which can't be good for their education. Why do the marks in the final examination cluster so monotonously about the middle of the second class instead of distributing themselves satisfyingly from extreme to extreme? What do the undergraduates think? The external examiners have ordered us in future to do Y (they do Y at their own universities and it works well enough) but, unfortunately, our Decrees are such that we'd need an Act of Parliament to be allowed to do Y. Here's a good idea, why don't we make our teaching very broad-based like they do at Budleigh Salterton? Excellent suggestion, and let's make it simultaneously very deep like they did at my old university. What do the undergraduates think?

This is all familiar enough – and laudable enough, for, despite my opening cynicism, there is certainly much that could be improved and it is undoubtedly our duty to seek it out. But one particular suggestion which has started to emerge recently has got to the roots of my hackles. Our teaching has been accused of being 'tutorial-driven.' The phrase originated with a pair of external examiners, who have been egged on to perceive their brief as widened from commenting on our examination to telling us how to run our University. It has been dutifully taken up by junior and senior members of Joint Consultative Committees, and is now echoing around departmental corridors. Our teaching is 'tutorial-driven' where it should be 'lecture-driven.' The meaning of tutorial-driven is best explained by reference to its remedy. The content of tutorial essays should be strictly limited to topics covered in official lectures. Tutors must be told the content of the lectures and must 'address' (to use the pretentious golfing jargon) these topics in their tutorials. Perhaps lecturers should distribute reading lists which all tutors must adopt and assign to their pupils.

I'll tell you what makes me so particularly sad about this philistinism. I was an undergraduate myself once; we were tutorial-driven (we didn't realise it at the time) and it has been the making of my whole life. Not just one particular tutor: it was the whole experience of the Oxford tutorial system and that *means* tutorial-driven. In my penultimate term Peter Brunet, my wise and humane college tutor, managed to secure for me tutorials in Animal Behaviour with the great Niko Tinbergen, later to win the Nobel Prize for his part in founding the science of ethology. Tinbergen himself was solely responsible for all the lectures in Animal Behaviour, so he would have been well-placed to give 'lecture-driven' tutorials. I need hardly say that he did no such thing. Each week my tutorial assignment was to read one D.Phil thesis. My essay was to be a combination of D.Phil examiner's report, proposal for follow-up research, review of the history of the subject in which the thesis fell, and theoretical and philosophical discussion of the issues that the thesis raised. Never for one moment did it occur to either of us to wonder whether this assignment would be directly useful to me in answering some exam question. We might have thought that it might have been useful to me in whatever career I eventually undertook.

Another term my college tutor, recognizing that my bias in biology was more philosophical than his own, arranged for me to have tutorials with Arthur Cain, an effervescently brilliant young star of the department, who went on to become Professor of Zoology at Liverpool. Far from his tutorials being driven by any lectures then being offered for the Honour School of Zoology, Cain had me reading nothing but books on history and philosophy. It was up to me to work out the connections between zoology and the books that I was reading. I tried, and I loved the trying. I'm not saying that my juvenile essays in the philosophy of biology were any good – with hindsight I know that they were not – but I do know that I have never forgotten the exhilaration of writing them.

The same is true of my more mainline essays on standard zoological topics. I have not the slightest memory of whether we had a lecture on the water-vascular system of starfish. Probably we did, but I am happy to say that the fact had no bearing upon my tutor's decision to assign an essay on the topic. The starfish water vascular system is one of many highly specialised topics in zoology that I now recall for the same reason – that I wrote an essay on them. Starfish don't have red blood, they have piped sea water instead. Sea-water enters through a hole, and is constantly being circulated through an intricate system of tubes which form a ring around the centre of the star and lead off in branches down each of the five arms. The piped sea water embodies a unique hydraulic pressure system, operating the many hundreds of tiny tube feet arrayed along the five arms. Each tube foot ends in a little gripping sucker, and they grope and swing back and forth in collusion to pull the starfish along in a particular direction. The tube feet don't move in unison but are semi-autonomous and, if the circum-oral nerve ring that gives them their orders should chance to become severed, the tube feet in different arms can pull in opposite directions and tear the starfish in half.

I remember the bare facts about starfish hydraulics but it is not the facts that matter. What matters is the way in which we were encouraged to find them. We didn't just mug up a textbook, we went into the library and looked up books old and new; we followed trails of original research papers until we had made ourselves as near world-authorities on the topic at hand as it is possible to become in one week. The encouragement provided by the weekly tutorial meant that one didn't just read about starfish hydraulics, or whatever the topic was. For that one week I remember that I slept, ate and dreamed starfish hydraulics. Tube feet marched behind my eyelids, hydraulic pedicellariae quested and sea water pulsed through my dozing brain. Writing my essay was the catharsis, and the tutorial was the justification for the entire week. And then the next week there would be a new topic and a new feast of images to be conjured in the library. We were being educated and our education was tutorial-driven.

I don't mean to knock lectures. Lectures, too, can be inspiring, especially when the lecturer throws away utilitarian preoccupations with syllabuses and with 'imparting information.' No zoologist of my generation will forget Sir Alister Hardy's lightning works of art on the blackboard, his recitations of comic verse on larval forms and his mimed imitations of their antics, nor his evocation of the blooming plankton fields of the open sea. Others who took a more cerebral and less pyrotechnic approach were just as good in their way. But, however good the lectures, we didn't ask for our tutorials to be driven by them and we didn't expect our exam questions to be lecture-driven either. The whole field of zoology was fair game for the examiners and the only thing we could rely upon was a presumption that our question papers would not be too unfairly different from their recent predecessors. The examiners when setting the papers, and our tutors when handing out essay topics, neither knew nor cared which subjects had been covered in lectures.

Well yes, of course I have just been indulging in a different kind of orgy, an orgy of nostalgia for my own university and its possibly unique method of education. I have no right to assume that the system under which I was educated is the best, any more than my incoming colleagues have a right to make the reciprocal assumption about their own excellent universities. We have to make individual arguments for the educational merits of whatever systems we wish to advocate. We must not assume that, because something is traditionally done at Oxford it is necessarily good (it is, in any case, amazing how *recent* most so-called ancient traditions often turn out to be). But also we must beware of the opposite assumption that because something is traditionally done at Oxford it therefore is self-evidently bad. It is on its educational merits alone that I am prepared to argue the case that our Oxford education should continue to be 'tutorial-driven.' Or if it is not to be, and we decide to abolish the tutorial system, then let us at least know what it is that we are abolishing. If we replace the Oxford tutorial, let us do so in spite of its glories and because we think we have found something better, *not* because we never properly understood what a real tutorial was in the first place.

6. Tutorials in Greats and History: The Socratic Method
Robin Lane Fox, Fellow in Ancient History, New College

The Oxford Tutorial brings one or two pupils into contact with a single teacher in their subject. There are off days, and occasionally a teacher or pupil does not, or cannot, try. The off days, which are rare, are not the measure of the system. It is not just a source of information, of which there are so many sources, on and off line. It aims to teach pupils something else: to think.

Subjects may vary, and so may their different branches, in the degree to which they require critical thought. My own subject, ancient history, depends on it. Its four-year degree, 'Greats', has a very special relationship with the Oxford Tutorial: it shaped its method. 'Greats' is not just a course in Classics. Until 1970, philosophy, both ancient and modern, was a compulsory half of the last two years' study. Even now, many candidates still choose it. Study of Plato's dialogues was obligatory, therefore, for some of Oxford's most famous tutors and pupils for about a hundred years. These dialogues also portray a sort of tutorial, the procedure of Socrates with young protagonists. Oxford tutors' set texts and their weekly practice thus seemed to belong in harmony. Because of 'Greats' the Oxford Tutorial was widely believed to pursue the 'Socratic method'.

The belief still persists, and it might seem too neat to be cogent. Greek thinkers before Socrates had already been aware that our ideals may simply be projections of what we know best in the world around us. An animal, a cow for instance, will imagine its god to be a cow; a barbarian Thracian will imagine his god to look like a Thracian. The first part of this insight has, in fact, been challenged by a leading Oxford Classicist: his cat, he has claimed, would imagine God to be like himself, the cat's master, who feeds and cares for it, and not like another cat, written large in heaven. Nonetheless, the insight is often true. When teachers were focussed on texts about Socrates's teaching, were they not likely to imagine that the ideal Tutorial was one carried out in Socrates's own style?

I wish to argue here that there is far more to the 'Socratic ideal' than an unthinking projection of our own practice into an ideal type. There is, however, a preliminary difficulty: which phase of the 'Socratic method' is the ideal? In Socrates's *Apology*, written so beautifully after his death by Plato, Socrates is made to say that his happy expectation of an after-life is a life spent perpetually in tutorial discussion with pupils beyond the grave. Modern exponents of 'Socratic teaching' may shudder at the thought. In the after life, however, eternity would exclude changes in Socrates's own level of stamina and patient commitment. The question, rather, is what this teaching would be. In this world, Plato's depiction of Socrates alters over time. In the early dialogues, handsome members of the *jeunesse dorée* in Athens present Socrates with everyday working definitions of central concepts in human life. Justice, for instance, is said to be 'giving each his due', whereupon Socrates goes back to what might be 'basics' and leads his young pupil obliquely by questions and answers until the pupil's confusions and contradictions are exposed and the working definition turns out to be unworkable. Then, the pupil, another pupil or Socrates tries all over again.

The pupils are always male, often handsome and usually the sons of very rich and well-born families. Here, the Socratic setting is no longer Oxford's. The method, however, is the one which tutors professed as their aim. By questioning, a pupil is led to an impasse from which he realizes the error of his starting point. The method pre-supposes a direct contact between teacher and pupil, one to one with, at most, two or three onlookers waiting to enter the fray. In this phase, Socrates tends to focus on one pupil at a time, taking him individually through a path which exposes his mistakes. He does not argue simultaneously with three or four, in a conference or class.

As almost every reader of Plato soon realizes, there is another similarity with most people's 'tutorial experience': Plato's Socrates is allowed to get away with some extraordinarily bad arguments. The reasons for this intellectual skating are still disputed. Was Plato testing his readers by these bad arguments and was he using them early on in long works like his *Republic* in order to sharpen his public's logical skills? Whatever the answer (I am unsure about these ones), there is an overlap here too with Oxford tutors. Not even the best of them is infallible and, in fact, they are being most 'Socratic', though they probably never see it this way, when they are teaching something which is not entirely cogent or when, as we all do, they hurry over thin ice without realizing that they do so. It is a further Socratic lesson of importance which tutorials pass on.

In later life, Plato presented a different 'Socratic method' altogether. His Socrates still starts in discussion with another person, but he gives up the business of step by step questioning and simply drones on for what we now read as page after page. Occasionally he pauses to ask the pupil if he agrees, but all the pupil is allowed to say is "How not, O Socrates?" This method, too, is Socratic, and so proponents of the 'tutorial method' need to be clear which 'Socratic method' they are following: the early one, or the late?

Here, I would like to be autobiographical. When I first studied ancient history, especially Greek history, which I now teach, "How not, O Socrates?" was for nearly two years the overriding 'method' which I acquired. In the first of these years, my inexhaustible and deeply inspiring tutor would gather his pupils together in small groups of three or four and expound to them at length, and in advance, the views on the topic for their next week's essay which he himself held and which he wished them to reproduce. "How not?", I thought, partly impressed and always glad of a short cut. When we handed in our essays on these general lines, the weekly tutorial consisted of being given them back, heavy with written comments. Our scrupulous tutor would then pick up one or two points where one or other of us had departed from his advance warning of what to think. He would put them on the right lines and then, perhaps in case we were forgetful, he would imitate the later Socrates and repeat his fully-developed views all over again.

In my second year, my second tutor proceeded differently, but not with such a different result as you might think. He, too, would call us together in advance, describing these sessions as 'briefings' but limiting them to setting a topic, suggesting a very few items of bibliography and then framing, or hinting at, questions which we should ask ourselves. This last point was new to me, but admirably true to his own former tutor, the great R.G. Collingwood, the last Oxford Professor to have excelled in both philosophy and ancient history. Collingwood had an extremely fertile philosophy of history which stressed the essential subjectivity of the study, partly in the sense that it was for the historian himself to begin by framing a question. As my own tutor used to put it, "the historian is only as good as the question he asks". I remain grateful for this important observation and try to pass it on.

When a pupil returned with an essay, he read it out to the tutor and a process of questioning, with scope for answers, followed. "How wonderfully Socratic and Phase One", you may be thinking, but in fact it was Phase Two in a barely-concealed way. No essay could ever contain the extreme ingenuities, insights and hobby-horses which our old and experienced tutor had constructed over so many years. Unlike Socrates, his questioning did not lend us to see the errors of our essays and leave us as agnostics. It began where we left off and led us down a new path, point by point to our tutor's own inexorable views instead. They were backed up by a non-Socratic aid: well-worn copies of ancient 'sources' which were put under our noses and appeared to clinch the point at issue. They were supported by frequent assertions of the teacher's own cleverness. These assertions, however, were interposed by the teacher himself. Even the Phase Two Socrates remained ironic enough to avoid this trap. Then the tutor would conclude "the question is not *whether* your tutor is clever, but *why* he is so clever". This final remark was actually an important encouragement to method and subjectivity, but we did not go into more detail. "How not, O Socrates?" had intervened and once again become my grateful response. Here too, I learned an awful amount which was new, some of which (in true Socratic style) turns out to be false.

The 'Socratic method' in my Oxford experience was the method of Phase Two. The first of my tutors was admirably explicit on the point. When I was appointed to succeed him, he told me that "many people in Oxford" will tell you that the tutorial uses the Socratic method, but "I advise you only to imitate the Socrates of the later dialogues". I was, however, a divided soul.

On the one hand, I realized that I had learned a remarkable amount from Phase Two tutorials, both factually and also procedurally. They were indoctrination sessions, but not without reasoned, decisive argument against other scholar's views; 'refutations' which were, and remain, entirely cogent. I had gained a remarkably wide and thorough grasp of the evidence and 'answers' to each topic. I had also gained an invaluable sense, not lost since, that historians can make progress by ruling out other historians' indefensible views and that, inch by inch, they are also advancing by excluding error. This awareness preceded later counter-currents, the onset of relativism, the rise of deconstructionism and the attempted reductions of history to nothing but plausible rhetoric. It has sustained me in sharp retorts to all these false turnings ever since. The Phase Two years have also been more positive. When starting a new and alien subject, forced on us by a syllabus, we are actually very glad of a solid body of information, most of which is knowledge. If it is imparted verbally by a forceful, unusual personality in a small group, it makes a much more vivid and lasting impression than if it is given in a lecture, backed up by an intimidating 'hand-out' on a bit of paper, or played on a cassette.

On the other hand, the Phase Two years had pandered to my own cunning and skilled short-cutting. Other people turned out to have been tutored in a Phase One mode only, and encounters with them posed serious problems for me. When they applied Phase One techniques to what I believed to be Phase Two's 'final solution', I tended to flounder. I also now realize that, unwittingly, I steered away for many years from other tutorial periods in which I had not had the benefit of Phase Two teaching. There was an answer to each topic, I believed, and a teeming load of non-answers, but, as no Phase Two practitioner had yet told me them, it would be a long, and probably fruitless, effort to try to construct them myself.

Like every former pupil who suddenly becomes a tutor, I decided to improve the method which had once formed me, adopting the good bits, revising others. I would essentially follow Phase Two, but try to make it less exhausting. So, after two years' debilitating practice, I asked a Headmaster, a great name in Education Theory, how he advised that a tutorial should become less one-sided. "You ask the pupil a question?", he inquired, and, when I said I did, he advised me that the problem was that I did not wait long enough for the pupil to come up with an answer. His research implied that tutors jump in too soon. Fluent Plato, of course, had elided the pauses on our printed pages: I accepted that it would be more genuinely Socratic to go back and ask, and wait.

Enthused, I went back for the first post-lunch tutorial, a low point in the Oxford day which is only beaten by a lower one, the second session after lunch. An amiable pair came in, one of whom read an essay on the beginnings of democracy in Athens and I asked him a question about the role, or non-role, of Athens's supreme Council, the Areopagus. There was the usual half-minute's silence, but this time I waited for a two-minute silence, then for three. Nothing happened, except that the other member of the tutorial began to write in his essay's margin. Nobody spoke, until I did, and then morale seemed to revive. When I took in the other, unread essay, I looked for the thoughts in the margin, wondering if I had scared them off. They simply said, "Buy Fairy Liquid; ring Claudia". The belief that an answer is always waiting, but that it takes time to form, is educationally false.

Since then, I have tried to compromise between Phase One and Phase Two, varying in emphasis until it is perhaps not for me to pronounce on its success. This long Odyssey may seem, at first, to be a poor advertisement for Socratic teaching: what else is his method but a negative attempt to undermine people and leave nothing behind but ignorance, or an indoctrination which inspires a routine "How not?". Plato's Socrates also holds some very curious views on foreknowledge, as if each one of us carries knowledge from a previous existence which can surface when confronted with a new problem. I very much doubt it, but, even if they do, a long wait after a question is never going to re-activate it.

Yet, there are other 'Socratic' virtues which still validate the process. Nowadays, most history-tutors probably mix a Phase One style with a bout of Phase Two which is helpful. The underlying strengths of a tutorial thus flourish in these days of compromise. Each week, a pupil has to work through a question for himself, put together an argued case and (in my tutorials) deliver it verbally. Unlike a lecture, this experience forces him to commit himself and go through the supporting evidence in person. He has to reach a view, identify himself with it, and express it, which is an art in itself and exposes those who have copied something out without appropriating it at all. Just as we cannot learn to play the piano by listening to others playing well, so we learn to argue a historical case by going through it and arguing it ourselves. There are, of course, items in life of which we have knowledge without going through this personal inquiry and engagement (our parentage, for instance, which we know without requiring ourselves or our parents to go through the act of creating us, with us or in our presence). But history is not just a matter of knowledge. It requires the personal asking of a question, a logical argument, the weighing of evidence and the use of it.

These arts are Socratic: in his mixture of Socrates One and Socrates Two, the tutor is conducting a master-class and helping the pupil to improve his own skill and performance. The skills which this process teaches are transferable. The presentation of an argument, the defence of this argument (rather than a question-begging narrative) and its use of evidence can be carried over from any period of history to another. It is an empowerment to range widely, not (as in my case) a deterrent from mainstream waters. It can be transferred to other settings, to decisions over how, or where, to live, how to understand the experience of travel and even (to our funders' relief) how to run a business or make money. Listening to a lecture may teach you something (but not all) about how to give a better lecture, but it will not teach you a method or how to interpret history by yourself.

To be capable of it, you have to do it: the more often you do it on more varied topics, the better you become at it. Part of 'it' is presenting an argument, and, if the recipient then argues back, in a direct personal engagement, the argument is much more likely to be tested and refined. The bigger the group, the less the engagement by each member and the less these consequences follow. As a result, there is less of a personally-appropriated method which can be transferred elsewhere.

It is ironic that those who wish to 'increase through-put' and cut out this costly, patient process are actually putting the clock back to the 1830s. So far from 'modernizing', they are returning the next generation to a plight which is excellently described by Mark Pattison, eventual Rector of Lincoln, in his *Memoirs*. In the 1830s he found "Young MA's of talent are all taken up with the conduct of some wheel in the complex machinery of cram which grinds down all specific tendencies and tastes into one uniform mediocrity..." The young Mark Pattison never had a tutorial, in the sense of a personal encounter with a mixture of Socratic Phases One and Two. Instead he realized the dream of many modern 'rationalizers' and went to nothing but lectures, before hiring a 'coach', "one of those routine professionals who just supply your memory with the received solutions of the patent difficulties of philosophy, as current in the Schools." The aim was to do well in exams ('Schools' or 'Finals'), the aim which is nowadays touted in 'League Tables' and in measures of 'Value Added' as the index of success. "I rushed into the Schools and only just saved my second....": as a victim of the system which 'modernizers' wish to dredge back from the past, this inquiring and widely-read entrant ended up in disillusion and unmethodical disarray.

Lectures teach you to take notes while the mind tries to wander, and then to recycle the outcome: tutorials oblige you to think. In Mark Pattison's view, the tutors were not often engaged, either: "In matter of fact, a tutor often did no more than half of what the class could have done quite as well". Nobody could answer back or begin by expressing new views or put the tutor on the mat. In our College library copy, a pencil note has been added, 'I see things have not changed'. But a few quips and a few bad tutorials do not negate the value of the Oxford Tutorial as an institution.

There is also, of course, the personal contact. Nowadays, it is formally and strictly regulated, as it always was by the inner code of conscientious people. Once a week, it gives a pupil a personal encounter, punctually conducted (usually) with an older, interested mind. Socrates used to love his pupils, and it is still entirely possible to love a pupil's mind and for both to thrive on that love. Socrates had beautiful pupils too, all males, and so a suspiciously large literature developed to rebut, by implication, that he was guilty of sexual harassment. In general, I accept that he was not. In a rather broader sense, a modern tutorial is therapeutic: each side is enlarged by the other's nuances of thought and presentation. Of course, there are whole areas which each person never knows about his partner. But each of them knows the quality of each other's mind, and though its application may vary in the future, that quality tends to endure. Even in a Phase Two session, this knowledge is something that every participant, however apparently reticent, carries away.

The transferable skills of asking a question, assessing the evidence for an answer and then presenting it personally are rare and should never be endangered. So, too, is learning to think while also learning how others think, and learning that even the most authoritative thinkers are fallible and, sometimes, wrong. The Athenians made a dreadful mistake and eventually condemned Socrates to death. You can kill a tutor, or wish he was dead, but you cannot kill Socratic methods. The tutorial may one day be martyred by others in ignorance, but it is not the guilty party.

7. Engineering the Tutorial Experience
Penny Probert Smith, Fellow in Engineering Science, Lady Margaret Hall

A little history
In terms of size and revenue, science and engineering are highly significant to the University. However, in terms of its history they are but newcomers. The structure and methods of tutorial teaching were established well before they came onto the scene. Yet in spite of the provision of lectures and practicals by the University departments, the tutorial retains a central position in the teaching of Oxford sciences. To understand how this has evolved perhaps it is useful to look back a while.

The first of the Oxford colleges was established in the thirteenth century. The colleges were founded as communities of scholars: *devoted to the study of letters ... Care and a diligent solicitude must be taken that no persons be admitted but those who are of good conduct, chaste, peaceable, humble, indigent, of ability for study, and desirous of improvement... Some of the discreetest of the Scholars [are] to be selected; and they... must undertake the care of the younger sort and see to their proficiency in study and good behaviour.*
(Taken from the Statutes of Merton, as quoted in *The Oxford Book of Oxford*, Jan Morris, 1984)

Recognise yourselves? Seven centuries later the colleges remain, and so does the concept of a scholarly community, but the role of instruction has been extended and formalised in the dual communities of tutors and undergraduates (there is also, of course, a graduate community of those reading for higher degrees but we will not discuss this here). The onus of care in the proficiency of study is realised, at collegiate level, in the tutorial system.

Since those days there have been many changes. By the eighteenth century academic standards had become, in many areas, secondary to social standing and high life. Tutorial instruction was haphazard (and so, it seems were examinations, which were entirely oral). There were many conscientious tutors, but others too. Many undergraduates were 'gentlemen commoners', at Oxford solely for the purpose of social advancement. Epitaphs of the eighteenth century include one to a Fellow of All Souls:

> *Here lyes Dr Sargeant within these cloisters*
> *Whom, if the last trump don't wake, then crye oysters*

and to one of Oriel ..

> *Here lies Randal Peter*
> *Of Oriel, the eater*
> *Whom death at last has eaten*
> *Thus is the biter bitten*

The great changes came in the mid-nineteenth century, forced by an act of parliament. The University was reformed into an institution which was intellectually vigorous on a world stage, and access started to be opened out as some of the worst class-distinctions were removed. In the same century the sciences were introduced. In the 1850s work began on the University Museum (in Parks Road), which was intended to be a fulcrum for scientific life in Oxford. Over succeeding decades this was followed by a wave of University building: the establishment of the University science area stretching along Parks Road (engineering) and South Parks Road. Now it stretches out beyond the ring road.

The Science University
But science left a greater mark on the University than just new buildings. It heralded the change to new loyalties. Suddenly the University had central science facilities and tutors were appointed who spent much of their time in laboratories away from college. The University departmental structure evolved to form a new structure for teaching and research existing side by side with the colleges in the University.

Superficially the world of science and engineering today has no connection with the federation of colleges of early Oxford. Many tutors work in close partnership with industry or other institutions and are responsible for large research budgets; a number own businesses to market their research. Tutors from all colleges come together in their Department as University lecturers, readers and professors, to deliver central teaching – lectures and practical classes (and examinations) – across all colleges. Tutors spend much of their working life in the Department, dashing into college for lunch, meetings and to see you. You too will spend much of your working day in your Department. However, the importance of the college remains. Your college tutor will oversee and advise you both academically and, if necessary, pastorally. The importance of college teaching is reflected in the fact that it is tutorials, rather than lectures, that are compulsory. If you do not attend lectures, you will be expected to acquire the information some other way (through your own reading); if you do not attend tutorials you will be up on disciplinary charges. The college is still likely to be the centre of your existence, both socially and academically, and (just as for Arts students) it is to the college that most Oxford graduates see their primary allegiance.

In the social side this will be because of friendships. On the academic side it will probably because of your relationship with your tutors. Most colleges have one or two tutors in each subject, and sometimes a college lecturer (someone who gives tutorials but is part-time and usually on a temporary contract). You probably saw your tutors at interview; you will almost certainly be tutored primarily by them in your first year or two. You will see them from time to time in the Department too in their University role.

As specialisation advances the pattern of teaching changes in most of the sciences: for example, in engineering we teach in classes for much of the third and fourth years. But the emphasis on individual teaching does not die out. Instead the tutorial transmogrifies into project supervision, possibly with your own tutor but most probably with one from another college (since projects are chosen according to subject interest, not college). However, this essay is about the beginning of your Oxford career and we will concentrate on the tutorial.

The value of 'the lecture'

No course in Oxford is lecture intensive but most cover a lot of material. Lectures are the first pass through it. They provide a coherent look and detailed introduction, including descriptive and analytical ideas, and are normally accompanied by copious printed notes with recommendations for further reading. They often provide links to research material, to commercial application and some analytical examples. They are scrutinised by panels of lecturers, and formal feedback from undergraduates is requested. However, although questions are normally welcomed, they are not by nature interactive because group sizes are so large (commonly over one hundred). Although lecturers prepare carefully, students often see the lecture simply as a chance to sit back and soak up knowledge, and, although they do not gain as much as they might by this view, the lecture can still fulfill one of its purposes, which is the transfer of information. Even the conscientious are not expected to assimilate all the material presented during the lecture; it is given to be thought about and mulled over in your own time. You do not see an individual lecturer all that often, maybe just for twice a week for a few weeks of your time in Oxford (more when you specialise in your final years). In some sense lectures are the stuff of quality assurance. At the start of a lecture the material to be covered is stated; the end can be written even before the lecture is presented. They are presented in public, open to all.

Tutorials are different

They are private events, usually taking place in the tutor's office in college or department. Your tutors provide continuity and a personal touch; you will see them regularly and get to know them very well. The tutorial emphasises the individual, both tutor and undergraduate. The end cannot be pre-determined beforehand because the tutorial responds to need. All must participate for it to be meaningful. You will be set work for each tutorial, normally questions based closely on the lectures. If you do not do these, the tutorial will be a waste of time for everyone. The preparation you make is your chance to take the material you've been lectured on and make it your own.

At its best, education is a 'leading out', not a 'cramming in'. More than ever before, however, an emphasis on examinations has pervaded the whole of education, from primary level upwards and distorted its meaning. Revision guides proliferate, with, at GCSE, headings such as 'All you need to know on light', followed by perhaps twenty facts and formulae. Examinations must have their place as a method to extend and test understanding, but education is much more than a cramming exercise, and light (and other phenomena) more than twenty facts. Yet this perception can be retained right through university too. Typical quotes from students in a Physics Department (not Oxford, but we are not blameless) include comments such as the following:

All we do is learn equations. The way to answer a question is just to decide which equation to use and plug it in. We never get the chance to understand what is going on

This is certainly not the aim of staff, who are academics because of their love for a subject. However, clearly there is a problem here. How do you balance the provision of information with the development of understanding? Perhaps the student view is sometimes reinforced by the emphasis on analytical questions for tutorial work. These are necessary; analysis and understanding feed off one another. But tutorials are much more than an examples class with the primary aim of providing solutions. They offer the chance to progress from a surface understanding to a deeper knowledge of what is really going on. The tutor's job is to ask the questions, stimulate the discussion, and provide the guidance to help you to deepen both conceptual understanding and analytical technique. But do not ever under-estimate the effort required from you in the process; it may not be an easy transition.

Just attending a tutorial will not get you far. It might (and should) give you solutions to any questions you can't grasp; it might provide a chunk of useful background material, a resume of particular techniques. However, if you have not done you part in preparation and made a serious attempt on your own to come to grips with the material to be covered, you will not know the right questions to ask and you will not be able to handle the quantity of material which is discussed. Although sometimes they take this role, tutorials are not primarily remedial. Nor are they there to impart information; lectures and your own reading do this. Tutorials aim to challenge your understanding and hence to extend it.

Quality-control
The tutorial is not readily amenable to quality assurance exercises. Tutors come in all shapes and forms, and the tutorial has managed to retain its individuality, eluding, so far, the bureaucracy of standards-policing and of intrusive quality-control legislation. In Oxford all permanent academic staff tutor (apart from a few professors). Although you will be taught mainly by your college tutors at first, sometimes you will have tutorials from tutors in other colleges, perhaps by post-doctoral researchers, even by research students, who often strike up a very good rapport with undergraduates. Your tutor may have just been appointed; he may have many years experience. He is likely to be amongst world leaders in his own particular subject. He may teach you only in his own subject and offer great depth of insight, or perhaps across many subjects and be able to draw together threads right across the course. You will get to know your tutors' foibles, their strengths and weaknesses as time goes on (in the same way as they will yours), and you need to decide how best to make use of them. Tutorials are your opportunity to learn, not your tutor's. As long as you show a genuine interest and responsibility in your work, are responsive to suggestions and acknowledge their greater experience, most tutors will respond positively if you request that certain areas are dealt with.

The hardest people to tutor are those who say nothing and put no effort into the running of the session. Sometimes this is through lack of confidence but usually confidence grows quickly as you get to know the tutor (there are a few who retain a demi-god status, but this fortunately is rare). More frequently it is through idleness. But be warned: tutors may refuse to teach you if you have not done the preparation and most colleges will take disciplinary action against people who clearly are not working properly.

Traditionally the Oxford tutor was a generalist, able to cover everything. This was fine in the early days – especially in the era of poorly defined examinations – but unrealistic in the context of courses today. In the first year you are likely to find that a single tutor will cover around half the course but as time goes on you will gain extra tutors for particular courses. You can expect certain things from your tutor: he should be prepared to discuss the subject area generally, to be in a position to help with particular questions, and to suggest further reading and ideas for you to follow up. Sometimes, especially if teaching a subject which is not his specialisation, he may not be able to provide answers straight away. My experience is that undergraduates are normally quite pleased to find that they are not the only ones who find a question difficult! A Natural Science viva in the late nineteenth century is reported as follows:

> *Examiner: 'What is Electricity?'*
> *Candidate: 'Oh Sir, I'm sure I learnt what it is ... but I've forgotten.'*
> *Examiner: 'How very unfortunate. Only two persons have ever known what*
> *electricity is, the Author of Nature and yourself. Now one of the two*
> *has forgotten.'*
> (Falconer Madan, *Oxford Outside the Guide Books*, 1923)

So what actually happens?

Tutors may ask you questions to which they don't know the answer (but not in examinations)! Sometimes it is interesting and instructive to follow a line of reasoning brought up by an undergraduate even when it leads you both into uncharted territory. Never assume that the tutor knows everything!

All teaching is about relationships, but the tutorial works though a relationship which is far more personal than classes or lectures. Tutorials work best when everyone is relaxed enough to take risk, and to lose the fear of appearing foolish. Here they have a huge advantage over class teaching, since classes have a larger and often changing membership of people who do not know each other very well.

Tutorials may be testing but they are popular. My own students have praised them for two reasons. Both are really quite obvious.
- Making me work all year, not just for examinations: self-motivation can be hard to maintain over very long periods.
- Sorting out problems as they arise: essential in subjects which build up on earlier material, and reducing the problem of poor motivation which results from getting stuck with a problem at an early stage.

In the early days of Oxford, college tutors often saw their students daily for tuition and discussion. John Wesley (founder of Methodism) could not be faulted in his devotion to teaching since he commented in the 1730's:

> *I would have through myself little better than a highwayman if I had not teached them every day the year but Sundays.*

No eight week terms here! On the other hand Cardinal Newman (1817), who was clearly a conscientious student, wrote:

> *I went to the University with an active mind, and with no thought but that of hard reading; but when I got there I had as little tutorial assistance or guidance as is possible to conceive ...*

These days you will be relieved to hear that tutorial provision is not entirely a matter for the individual, and that there is active college overview to achieve a happy balance! You will probably have one or two tutorials a week, each for about an hour. The traditional tutorial is with just a single other undergraduate, your 'tutorial partner'. This style often works very well. There are surprisingly few mismatches between the tutorial partners and any that exist can usually be sorted out by re-grouping. Tutorials as a pair gives you both a chance to ask your individual questions, to be challenged by the questions from your partner, and to join in discussion actively. It gives you and your partner a chance to discuss problems before the tutorial and to run things together. Sometimes your tutor will run through solutions and explain material. Sometimes he will ask you to do that, especially as a response to the questions of your tutorial partner. There is nothing like trying to explain material to someone else to find out what you really understand! At other times you might be taken with all undergraduates in your year in college, probably for a longer period. The tutorial system encourages a close academic relationship between undergraduates in each college, something which they all benefit from as they are work together.

And what of the future?
Tutorials have many benefits, but the system is expensive in money and time. University funding relies heavily on research output, and there is increasing pressure on tutors to bring in research funding, with the corresponding responsibilities of project and financial management. External funding agencies do not recognise the demands of teaching. Your tutors are often harassed individuals, uneasily balanced between College and Department. Sometimes their preparation is not as good as it should be; sometimes you see them at the end of a long afternoon. *The days of port and peace are gone; I am a modern Oxford don* started a poem in the *Oxford Magazine* of 1894. Some of us feel like that a century later, bombarded by quality assessments, league tables and research project management.

Yet we still take tutorials very seriously. We enjoy the contact with you, the opportunity to get to know well a small group, to see you flourish as individuals both academically and personally over your time here. As teachers we treasure the moments when you say 'Yes! I understand that now'. It is good when you really challenge our own preconceptions and understanding. The blue liquid proffered to us at undergraduate cocktail parties, the horrors of the jokes session at undergraduate dinners, your amazement that, yes, we can still punt better than some of you in spite of our advanced years, perhaps forge a bond which helps us to counter the relentless burden of administration, and eases the pain of going through a solution for the fourth time that afternoon. We enjoy our incredulity when you turn up after many years, confident and responsible adults, as we remember your arrival as fearful or falsely sophisticated Freshers. It is a delight to have genuinely equal discussion on scientific and engineering topics with those of you who continue a career in science and technology, and to see you outstrip our own efforts.

But perhaps the greatest privilege of the tutor is the chance to share a little of our own fascination with our subjects, a chance which arises increasingly as you move through your career in Oxford.

And finally an admonitory story...

After the head of an Oxford college had given a public lecture, a little lady bustled up to him and enthused, 'Oh Master, that was splendid! Your topic was a subject about which I have always been confused!'

Pleased, he said 'And now you understand it better?'

'Not really', she replied, 'but I'm confused now on a higher level!'
(from *These Ruins are inhabited,* Muriel Beadsley, 1963)

There is nothing splendid about confusion. You are not to accept it, at whatever level. Individual rapport is vital to challenge and inspire, but also to elucidate. Although new pressures may cause the number of tutorials to diminish, the emphasis on individual development, on individual discussion, is dear to us all and will remain that way.

(NB. All unacknowledged quotations are taken from the *Oxford Book on Oxford*, Jan Morris, 1984.)

8. English: A Shared Enterprise

Emma Smith, Fellow in English, Hertford College

Maybe it's an occupational hazard, but, as a tutor in English, I'm particularly fascinated by the language of tutorial teaching. Do we talk, as tutors, of *giving* a tutorial (as if it were a bunch of flowers, perhaps, or some advice), or of *delivering* a tutorial (a parcel, or maybe a baby), or *teaching* a tutorial (as if it were a pupil)? Do we hold on to the older description of 'Stephen is *reading* Shakespeare with Dr Dee' which, as W.G. Moore recalls, was standard during the 1930s, with its quaint image of two coves in tweeds sitting over their books in companionable silence? Or do we instruct students to come for their tutorial as for a doctor's appointment – which, in a manner of speaking, I suppose it often is? And, as students, do we *have* tutorials (as if they were lift-off, or 'flu), or *go to* tutorials (attending, but are otherwise passive)? Cambridge University calls its tutorials 'supervisions' which suggests an activity at once more distant and more regulatory. I once wrote a card to arrange an initial meeting with a new student in which I used the phrase 'I'm looking forward to working with you on Marlowe this term'. This locution proved so confusing to the recipient that she settled on the idea that I was another, rather offputtingly formal and forward student, who would be paired with her during the term's tutorials with an as yet unidentified tutor.

But despite this lack of clarity, I'm holding onto 'working with' as, I think, the expression which most nearly captures my idea of good tutorial teaching. It contains the sense of joint effort, progress, and activity which characterises the most energising tutorials I've had, both as student and as tutor. The work tutor and student/s are together engaged in during the tutorial is both a general and shared enterprise – to develop different understandings of the texts in question – and a specific one – to extend individual student's work according to their particular strengths and areas for development. Tutorials can and should be dynamic, in the sense of moving and movable. No two tutorials should be the same, and no tutor should try and make them so. In this piece, which represents my own views but has been strengthened by the comments on earlier drafts by other colleagues in my Faculty, I want to outline what I, as a tutor, hope to achieve in tutorial teaching in my subject. I also want to suggest some of the reasons tutorials are not always as successful as they might be, and to propose some ways in which students might share more responsibility for, and thereby improve, the quality of their own tutorial experience.

The tutorial system is fundamentally opposed to the culture of conformity of teaching provision which reigns elsewhere in higher education. The only generally applicable advice for new students is to be flexible. Some tutors will require essays in advance, some will follow the pattern where one student reads out an essay and the other hands it in, some will have longer tutorials with larger groups. In some tutorials the focus is on an already completed piece of work, in others the work is yet to be completed and the tutorial is a kind of rain check. Some tutors will argue with students' work, some will dismantle it to show how it might have been done differently, some will take it as a starting point for a discussion of the topic. Some tutors may seem not to indicate what they think of the work, some will leave the student in no doubt about their assessment. Some tutorials will begin with the offer of coffee or with a general chat about matters non-academic, some will keep the agenda very much to the topic in hand. Some will involve work prescribed by the tutor, some will rely on a topic decided on and investigated by the student. You may have tutors within your college or outside it. You may be taught by a professor one term, and by a graduate student near completion of her D.Phil the next. Sometimes you may be taught on your own, sometimes in twos, rarely in groups of more than three. And so on. Some tutorials and some tutors will, inevitably, be more to individual students' tastes than others. Ask any group of students about their best tutor or tutorial and it's easy to see that you can't please all of the people all of the time. This variety is intrinsic to the Oxford tutorial system, and is thus both its greatest strength and, potentially, its great weakness. You will have some tutorials you enjoy more and gain more from than others.

In my tutorials, I'm trying to do several things, and, if even some of these objectives are achieved, I think that the tutorial has been worthwhile...

- To respond to students as individuals. In positive terms, they have a unique approach to their reading and research, and I want to help them develop the tools, confidence and knowledge to extend this. In more negative terms, they may have a particular difficulty or area of weakness, be it a sense of appropriate context or essay structure, and so may need specific, ongoing interventions into their work to reach their full potential.

- To monitor students' working habits and learning in between the tutorials – to check up on what they've read, how they found it, any difficulties or problems encountered, lectures or classes they've been to, and to discuss ways they might work more effectively, or more enjoyably, or just more.

- To convey my enthusiasm and excitement about my subject without presenting myself as someone who already knows it all, and therefore encourage students' own intellectual excitement.

- To encourage debate, discussion and the development of ideas within the tutorial, rather than to use the time simply to reflect or comment on ideas arrived at elsewhere.

- To attempt to connect work previously completed or still to be done, so as to monitor the more general points about the subject alongside the more specific ones.

- To draw together different kinds of teaching and learning, from faculty classes or lectures and from individual research, in order to situate the tutorial within this broader learning context.

- To set up work and joint expectations for the next meeting.

- To develop students' awareness of their ultimate assessment, by exam or whatever. This is a balancing act: I don't want to suggest that the sole purpose of tutorials is to prepare people for exams, but nor do I want there to be a great rift between the work covered in the tutorials and final exams. One of the best things about the English degree here at Oxford is that it is an education in literature in the widest sense: three years to read and think, not three years preparing to jump through some hoops in the final year.

While I couldn't really claim, despite the subtitle of this volume, that I have ever taught anyone how to think, I do try to provide a tutorial environment in which students' thinking – and my own – can be developed, challenged and encouraged.

Sometimes, of course, this doesn't work as I, or my students, would hope. On my side, sometimes I talk too much and don't let the student talk. Good listening is an often under-rated aspect of tutorial participation on both sides. Sometimes I don't feel the student is well-prepared, or that he is sufficiently interested in the topic to generate discussion, rather than simply field my questions. Sometimes students are exhausted with the effort of getting their essay finished in time, and the tutorial is a last half-waking hour before returning to bed to catch up on missed sleep. Sometimes two students don't seem to work well together, in which case I try to rearrange the groups. From the student point of view, there can be a feeling of frustration if the tutorial comes after the work for the essay has been completed, with a sense that if only they'd had this discussion earlier on they'd have been able to produce a more satisfying essay. I never give grades on marked work (although I do try to give the fullest possible feedback), but this can also leave students unsure about their progress. Tutorials, for me, are not about getting students to a particular standard and then saying 'that's fine', nor about encouraging students to compete for a higher mark, but about trying to extend and advance an individual student's work whatever standard he or she is currently reaching: it's as important to make suggestions for development on an essay which is of first class standard as it is for one which is third class.

What, then, can students do to improve their tutorials?

- Being well-prepared and reasonably rested helps, so that the tutorial can be an intensive period of reflection, reconsideration and discussion. If you are poorly prepared it's probably best to admit it and take the consequences. So long as you don't make a habit of it, this probably won't fatally impair your tutorial relationship (though you'll have to play a blinder next week!).

- Make sure you bring your notes and a copy of any relevant texts with you so that you can refer to them in the tutorial. Obviously a pen and paper are necessary: this is a developmental discussion from which you can take useful suggestions, not an interrogation.

• It's a good idea to have, even if not in a formalised way, a series of points, questions, issues you'd like to discuss so that you can take part-control of your tutorials and move along your own agenda. Being proactive – taking hold of the tutorial rather than submitting passively to it, is a way of getting more from the time spent.

• Practise active listening, both to the tutor and to the other student/s in the tutorial, and engage with, ask questions of, make observations about, what they are saying. Most tutors do like their own opinions, and arguably we all like the sound of our own voices, but more importantly all of us want participatory tutorials in which we can discuss the ideas we've committed our professional lives to with others who are keen to learn, argue, research and enjoy literature to the full.

Importantly, however, tutorials are not the only means of education in Oxford. They exist as part of a large number of different opportunities and the challenge for students is to make the most of each of these. As an English student, much of your time will be spent in individual, library-based research, in reading, thinking and taking notes. It's all the more important, therefore, that you take the opportunity to meet other people and get different perspectives whenever you can. Lectures offer an important overview of the syllabus and give you a chance to hear work in progress by expert scholars. You can also gain a broader sense of the period you are studying and different frameworks for your own individual research. It may be useful to bring back for discussion in your tutorials issues or questions or texts raised by lecturers. Faculty classes allow students from different colleges to get together to discuss, in small groups, a particular text or topic. At informal or occasional readings at student-run societies or bookshops you can hear about new work and the current literary scene. Your college may hold classes on different aspects of the syllabus. All of these, including tutorials, are crucially important in developing a broad range of approaches and skills, in being alerted to new ideas and sources of information, and in learning through interaction rather than just solitary reading.

Within this mixed teaching context, tutorials are the major means by which the 'working with' ethos of undergraduate teaching in English in the University is advanced. They offer a unique opportunity to develop, discuss and defend your literary judgements and pursue personal research with a high degree of individual attention. I hope you enjoy working with a range of tutors in a range of different ways during your Oxford career.

9. Perfection in Politics and Philosophy
Alan Ryan, Warden and formerly Fellow in Politics, New College, Oxford

When Socrates was told that he was the wisest man in Athens, he was puzzled. It seemed to him that he knew rather little. Indeed, about the matters that most concerned him, he thought he knew nothing. It finally struck him that he might have acquired a sort of wisdom; *nobody* knew anything, but he at least understood how ignorant he was. It was a dangerous doctrine. As it turned out, it was more dangerous to Socrates than to anyone else, since his fellow Athenians disliked having their conventional views of the gods challenged by Socrates's questioning, and shut him up by subjecting him to a trial for blasphemy and sentencing him to death.

Teaching politics and philosophy today is a great deal less dangerous than that. So is studying them. The process is, however, complicated in its own right, and complicated for both sides of the teaching exchange. Changes in what schools teach and how they teach it, as well as changes in what universities nowadays think the contents of a politics or philosophy syllabus should be have made a lot of difference to the undergraduate experience compared with even ten or fifteen years ago, let alone with forty years ago. How people teach in Oxford has changed at least as much. This is not the place to duplicate the PPE course handbook – an indispensable guide to everyday life – but to draw a quick sketch of a system in transition. I begin with what some people believe to have been a Golden Age, and others see as claustrophobic and complacent.

Imagine the perfect PPE student of 1960. He – in the Oxford of 1960 it is five to one that it is 'he' – has come from a traditional secondary school, maybe private, maybe direct grant; he has five O level passes – in English Language and Literature, Mathematics, French, and Latin. He may not have taken A level; if he had gained an entrance scholarship in the winter before he was due to sit A level, he could skip A level entirely. He might have stayed at school for as many as five terms after winning a scholarship, reading widely, writing gently, running the school debating society, and polishing his literary and investigative skills. When presented with formal logic in his first undergraduate term, he flinches for an instant, sees that it requires only a cool head and strong nerves, and polishes off little proofs as and when they are asked for. But this he does in classes taken alongside the tutorials that in those far off days defined the educational experience of the perfect student.

In the tutorial, the perfect student may or may not meet the perfect tutor; this does not much matter. For the perfect student has been reading Thucydides rather than Plato, and mediaeval history rather than Thomas Aquinas, and when first asked to decide whether our senses are chronically delusive, or whether Descartes' argument for the 'cogito' is sound, even the perfect student is much like Socrates's interlocutors, and decidedly puzzled about what sort of reply might constitute an answer. Here is where his school training comes to the rescue; knowing that he will not know what he thinks until he sees what he has written, he begins to write as soon as he opens the first article to which his tutor has directed him. This can on this first occasion be relied on to create more confusion than it will cure – though it remains in general a very good way to learn, since it anchors what one does know and brings to light what one does not. What mixture of intellectual insecurity, doubt and sudden illumination the perfect student endures during the three or four days he has been allotted for this first essay we cannot say, but the odds are that the experience has been intense and instructive. The perfect student will not have borrowed an essay from a second year student.

The next stage is the tutorial encounter. In 1960, it takes place one-to-one, in the tutor's study, the student gowned, in jacket and tie. The one thing the perfect student will have known all along is that when read out his essay must last no more than ten minutes, that it must make three (or at most four) points, and that it must make up in clarity for whatever it lacks in depth and sophistication. Now, the fate of the student is in the lap of – not the gods, but his tutor. Let us imagine that he has encountered the perfect tutor. This impossible creature has several possible manifestations; some tutors are perfect as only young teachers can be, and others in ways that only older teachers can manage. Some – my colleague Jonathan Glover was one – begin perfect and continue so, without the observer being able to say whether time has has made a difference to the astonishing personal skills they bring to the tutorial encounter.

Our fictional hero reads his essay. The perfect tutor is unlikely to interrupt; he has seen perfect students before and their essays have a pattern to them, and he need not hurry things. If he does interrupt, it will not be to correct a point or hand out information but because the perfect student has seen something interesting, difficult and obscure and both parties can abandon their stately progress through the topic and get their teeth into a single issue. Still, the perfect tutor will generally wait until the essay is concluded, and leave the best till last. What may slightly surprise the perfect student is that the tutor only speaks in questions; this is education by interrogation, and it does not matter how clumsy or halting the student's responses may be, since the object of the encounter is that the student should teach himself by understanding how to emerge from a spider's web of questions: "If you think *that*, then what do you want to say about…?". The perfect tutor does not succumb to the temptation to hand the student a quick summary of the five crucial things to remember about the topic in hand, does not mind long patches of thoughtful silence during the tutorial, and is confident that the student, being young, clever, and energetic, will teach himself everything he needs to know – so long as he is asked the right questions.

Tutorials in politics were similar, save for the fact that more facts might have been asked for, or at any rate some knowledge of them would have been presupposed in the discussion. The technique is simple to describe, though hard to implement: ask a seemingly simple question, provide some pointers to reading (but not an elaborate or detailed reading list, since part of the point of the exercise is to let students explore on their own behalf), make it clear that students *teach themselves* and that the tutor's task is to interrogate them in such a way as to discover how well they have taught themselves and in that way help them build up their ability to teach themselves.

There are several reasons why tutorials of this sort once worked very well as a form of education. One was that students had been writing essays since the age of six, and in many schools had had something close to tutorial instruction in the sixth form. They were used to working independently, and had had some practice in being treated as intellectual equals by their sixth form teachers. The classic tutorial was very much an Oxford institution; it was well suited to philosophy, politics, literary and historical subjects which were Oxford's strengths. In the physical sciences it perhaps used to work better, or at least more easily, than it does now. In the sciences, the frontier where currently accepted theories encounter hard to explain data is now metaphorically 'further away' from what a school student encounters than it was fifty or forty years ago. There is room for a great deal of methodological, historical, and pre-theoretical discussion in science education; and in some parts of the biological sciences the philosophical status of many theories is very much a live subject *within* rather than merely *about* the discipline.

It is less plausible to say this of the bulk of what an undergraduate today gets taught in chemistry, physics, and cognate disciplines. The effect is that open-ended argument as distinct from problem-solving is less salient than it once was. There have been many philosophical and sociological accounts of why this state of affairs exists – some suggest that it rests less on the reality of the growth of knowledge than on a sort of high-quality illusion, to which the discipline subscribes as a way of regulating itself.

Here, happily, we cannot and need not embroil ourselves in that discussion. All we need observe is that, *if* an education rests heavily on a training in technique and the accumulation of facts, it will not lend itself to fruitful egalitarian exchange of the sort that the tutorial is supposed to involve. It is sometimes said that when a discipline 'matures,' it inevitably becomes intellectually inegalitarian. The thought comes from T.S. Kuhn's essay, *The Structure of Scientific Revolutions,* which emphasizes the hierarchical structure of scientific communities where accredited experts determine the fate of research apprentices.

Kuhn drew the contrast I am relying on here. He was sure that humanities subjects were not 'immature' sciences, and sure that, whatever the social sciences might eventually become, they were not now mature sciences, and not immediately likely to turn into anything of the sort. But philosophy in the 1950s and 1960s had one feature of what Kuhn described as maturity – a consensus over the goals of the discipline and the methods of achieving them. Those who disliked the philosophy practised at the time complained that there was too much consensus over what the discipline was, what it aimed to do, and what methods were likely to be successful. But, the crucial difference between that sort of maturity and the maturity displayed in science was that everyone agreed that philosophy was not a technical discipline. The metaphorical distance between an absolute beginner with the right talent and temperament and the 'cutting edge' of philosophical inquiry was the length of a page. What distinguished tutors from their pupils was only that tutors had had more practice, more experience, had read rather more, and were more likely to know that some superficially attractive argument collapsed under pressure. But it was always possible – and often happened – that a really bright student would look at some piece of received wisdom and see immediately that it wouldn't wash at all.

There were further features of the consensus that with hindsight seem quite odd, but which made life easier for all concerned. One was the belief that all philosophical issues with any staying power could be handled as though they were being looked at for the first time by mid-20th century philosophers in the United Kingdom or on the East Coast of the United States. The assumption was that one could always translate whatever a thinker had *said* in some far off place, in some non-English language, or in a non-modern terminology, into the terms and concerns of post-1945 anglophone philosophers, thereby retrieving what he had *meant*. The question of how far one can do that is an interesting and difficult one that leads into philosohical complexities of its own. I think we all knew that at some level, but pretended not to in order to get on with what we really wanted to do.

Another feature of the consensus was that the range of things worth discussing was well-defined. As critics complained then and since, this shut out a lot of philosophers that other people thought were worth taking seriously. Sartre was acceptable as a novelist, but not in his own terms as a philosopher, so *Being and Nothingness* was read as an extended sketch of the plot of a series of novels. Heidegger was off the menu for every reason, and Nietzsche was left to poets and playwrights. This made it difficult to read Kant, since it was hard to deny that subsequent German Idealism had taken off from Kant, and hard to deny that Kant had in some fashion taken off from Hume as well as Leibniz. It was agreed that Kant was difficult but inescapable, as was Wittgenstein among the moderns.

Similarly, moral philosophy suffered from being over-shadowed by the preoccupation with the philosophy of language that dictated what were and what were not the central issues in philosophy. As to what became my own interests, political philosophy was rather less reputable than ethics, and the philosophy of the social sciences was yet to reappear from the grave in which Russell and Moore were generally thought to have buried the wretched John Stuart Mill and all his works. When these subjects did reappear, however, it was not by way of a revolution, but by pressing on the envelope of what had seemed respectable topics. The publication of Brian Barry's *Political Argument* of 1965 was a crucial step, although the pre-publication drafts of John Rawls's *A Theory of Justice*, which circulated from the early-1960s, made a lot of difference, too.

This Garden of Eden with all the blessings and deficiencies of the age of innocence was closed in the 1960s. Its great virtue for a student was that most people read the same things and understood the same arguments, however often they then came to different conclusions. When 'history' meant mostly English history from King Alfred to the outbreak of World War I, and 'politics' meant a little of the history of political thought and a lot of careful descriptions of the formal institutions of Britain, the United States, some European states and the Soviet Union, students read the same books as each other and their tutors, and tutorials were devoted to speculative interpretations of the common reading. Students got much of their education outside the library, lecture room and tutor's office; but a common core of reading, and a shared experience in the formal setting made informal mutual instruction easier and more coherent.

Into this cosy situation erupted – in no particular order – the cultural shake-up of the 1960s that saw rocketting divorce rates, the tripling of participation in higher education, the beginning of the long transition from a higher education population of eighteen year old boys to a population of mature students, part-time students, and a preponderance of women students, the politics of Vietnam and the student revolutions of 1968, the revival of Marxism and the first crumbling of the Soviet *bloc*, along with suddenly rising inflation, and what looked to many people by the middle of the 1970s like the simultaneous collapse of capitalist economies in the west and state socialism in the rest of the world.

Nobody knows what caused what; the effect was that many forms of consensus were suddenly challenged. With them went the intellectual authority of the educational institutions of the western world. If half the student body is high on the ecstatic hankerings of Herbert Marcuse, it does no good to announce that they are in the strict sense nonsense; that just disenchants the students with their elders and academic philosophy. If the young decide that Cuba holds the key to the transfiguration of political institutions and political authority, it is no use saying that sugar production dropped like a stone under Castro, and that Cuba was one of the few states to support the Soviet suppression of the Czech attempt to institute socialism with a human face.

For very large numbers of university teachers, the ten years from about 1964 to 1974 were deeply unsettling. For some, it was a liberation; others thought it was a re-run of the barbarian invasions and the end of civilization as they knew it. Happily, this essay need not take sides on that. All we need to acknowledge is that the content of syllabuses, intellectual authority, and forms of instruction were all thrown into the melting pot, and we can no longer rely on a consensus about what is worth studying and why. As usually happens after a revolution, the new world is a curious mixture of things that are absolutely different from what went before and things that are strikingly similar. The similarities can be depressing. Some students wander through university just as their predecessors did, learning enough to get the obligatory upper second, but begrudging any more intellectual effort than that. Like good Marxists – though they are not that – they think a purported exchange of ideas hides the extraction of surplus thinking. Other similarities are happier; students show up as frequently as ever who write with the verve of Bertrand Russell and argue with the seriousness of G.E. Moore – and others who have apparently been waiting all their lives to encounter Rousseau and experience the mixture of infatuation and rage proper to falling for someone as shifty, evasive and engrossing as he.

What is most different is the absence of a core experience. It is no longer true that the well-equipped philosophy or politics students will know a clearly defined range of core material along with much else. She or he will certainly know a great deal, but it is less predictable what it will be. Both the knowledge and the lacunae are much less predictable than they once were. Nor is the canonical intellectual encounter exactly what it was. The dazzling lecturer is less in demand; students wish to be enlightened rather than blinded. Nor do the faculty want to dazzle; they wish to instruct. The seminar is rightly more salient as a teaching vehicle and as a learning opportunity. It has always been true that students teach one another more than their teachers know how to teach them; and the seminar is generally and certainly more predictably a better vehicle for that than the cinema queue after a tutorial.

But one reason why the class and the seminar bulk larger is that the old assurance that students and tutors confront each other as equals has gone; so has the belief that anyone who has learned the basics can go on and teach herself the rest. Teachers feel they must give more instruction than they once did; the third year sixth form has vanished, so has the uniform content of an A level, and so has the examination regime based on constant essay writing. What therefore also bulks larger as a source of security is the official reading list. Because there are so many more special subjects to be covered, neither students nor teachers are confident that they know intuitively what a proper coverage looks like. The rise of academic professionalism makes a difference, too. Lectures attend more than they once did to the view within the profession about where an area of the discipline has got to, and students and their teachers are less willing to stray far off the line. It all makes for a much more reliable and predictable system of instruction than existed twenty, let alone forty, years ago. Whether it is as good for the cleverest and bravest students is hard to know; it certainly makes life very much better for students whose willingness to work is greater than their eagerness to take risks.

What is the profit and loss account? On the whole, progress has occurred. Although life is harder for anyone teaching philosophy and politics than it was forty years ago – mostly because of the increased quantity of record-keeping required today – it offers the satisfactions that come with a switch from an essentially amateur teaching system to something more professional. Most academics like teaching special subjects, and after a while get pretty fatigued teaching nothing but the core syllabus; the enormous increase in special subjects in both philosophy and politics is in that way all to the good. The range of discussable topics in both politics and philosophy has increased markedly, and that also must be all to the good. The compensation for the demise of (never more than a few) dazzling lectures is the rise of competent, non-boring, informative lectures at the end of which students know more than they did at the beginning. Most of what students lose by not keeping step with one another as they progress through the old-fashioned syllabus with few optional subjects, they gain by seeing more of each other in classes and lectures where their interest can reasonably be assumed to be greater. The losses are as much style as substance – though the line between style and substance may in both political and intellectual life be narrower than in other areas. There has been a reduction in the verve with which eighteen year olds contradict their fifty year old teachers; what they do when they are bright and demanding graduate students is not quite the same. Flair is less in demand and less in evidence as a result.

In short, most students will get an educational experience whose seriousness is guaranteed. It won't be the experience described by Stephen Leacock, who analysed tutorials as a process in which a tutor with a pipe 'smoked' the student for three years, nor will it be quite the process of forty years ago. But it will still involve writing vastly more essays than are demanded anywhere other than at Cambridge; it will involve innumerable occasions when you will have to defend what you have written; it is still education by interrogation – in which students learn how to ask themselves what they really think by being asked over and over again by those who are teaching what they really think about the subject at hand.

10. Tutorial Teaching in Economics

Richard Mash, Fellow in Economics, New College

What are economics tutorials for? How do they relate to other forms of teaching and learning? Are they useful – or more precisely when are they useful? Are they an outdated residue of some *ancien regime* or an integral part of a fully modern first-rate university education? Perhaps most importantly, how should students approach tutorials to maximise their usefulness? What follows are some personal reflections on these questions with a view to both the student reader wondering what tutorials are all about and the wider debate about their future. To anticipate, my view is that at their best tutorials are a fully contemporary form of teaching and learning that offer almost unique benefits – but getting the most out of them requires a lot from students, tutors and the teaching system as a whole.

To set the context it may be helpful to sketch what the process of learning and thinking about economics looks like overall. The starting point for work in the subject is the study of very simplified theoretical 'models' (representations) of the economy or parts of it, which is broadly what is covered in first-year work. Following this, in work geared towards Finals, are: i) the study of more complex (and realistic) theory models; ii) empirical applications of those models, in the sense of both using the models to interpret real world data and, in reverse, seeing what the data can tell us about the possible validity of the models; iii) assessment of policy issues; and iv) all of the above in different specialist areas covered by option papers. Ideally at the end of the process a Finalist has a good grasp of general economic theory, a sense of how to use it to assess and explain empirical evidence, and knowledge of some specialist areas; plus the ability to 'think like an economist' and a feel for where the research frontier is in at least some parts of the subject.

That is an outline of the intellectual process, which might be summarised as "sort out the basics and then move beyond them", but there is also the important dimension of how interesting and enjoyable the material is. In a nutshell the 'basics' can be quite interesting in themselves but the real interest and excitement lies beyond. Hence part of the challenge is to sort out the basics as quickly as possible – but without superficiality since they are essential to what follows.

How are students meant to learn all this? On the teaching side most of the core material required is covered in lectures with tutorials (and small group classes later on) running in parallel. Learning opportunities obviously include these but also, crucially, the student's own reading and reflection, both in term-time and as far as possible in vacations also when the absence of immediate deadlines makes it much easier to think about the wider picture. Work, either for money or experience, and travel and other things are real (and reasonable) constraints on vacation reading but happy is the tutor who receives an email during the vacation saying, "I was reading x and got confused by y, could you point me in the right direction".

So what happens in tutorials? What are they for? Starting from a solely intellectual perspective, let me attempt to answer these by presenting in turn a summary of 'bad' and 'good' tutorials. **What happens in a bad tutorial?** The defining feature of what can go wrong is that other parts of the learning and teaching process have not functioned properly. Students have not been to lectures (either because they are lazy and hope that they can get by with just tutorials, or because the lectures were too weak to bother with), and nor have they done much reading or thinking on the topic: they simply cobble together an essay before walking into the tutorial. What happens? The rather irritated tutor ends up taking the students through the basic material to achieve some sort of minimal understanding with no time for the more interesting material that digs deeper. The tutor talks too much, since the students have little to say apart from the odd clarifying question, so it's not far off a lecture delivered in the most uneconomic way you can think of. It's not often like this (otherwise one would leave... or perhaps campaign for tutorials to be abolished and lectures made compulsory), but this is what happens when the rest of the process is *not* happening.

What is a good tutorial like? At the other end of the spectrum the students will have been to lectures of at least reasonable quality, read thoroughly, and ideally spent several hours chewing over the material before planning and writing their essays. At the start of the tutorial the students will have understood much (but very rarely all) of the basic material required, and will have at least begun to think about wider dimensions of the topic. The tutorial now has two functions; firstly, a 'topping-up' exercise on the basics, prompted either by students' questions ("It was OK overall but I found this bit difficult") or the tutor's response to the essays, whether read beforehand or read out ("Good essay but you skimped on such and such"). This part is crucial – without the basics sorted out there is little point in moving forward – and can take time even with well-prepared students, but all being well there is time for more, for the second function. What does 'more' mean? Some mixture of greater depth on the material itself, its relation to other topics or policy, and developing some thoughts on where research on the topic should go next (or at least a sense of what more complex literature not yet studied has to say). Economics is a very live subject with vigorous research agendas on all fronts and very little is entirely established, uncontroversial or fully satisfactory as it stands. You have to be on top of what there is before thinking about what might or should come next, but it is wonderful if a tutorial can push some way into this territory.

A further remark on the 'good' tutorial is that virtually all of it can be 'question and answer' or discussion based. This means that the learning becomes 'active', in the sense that the student is much more involved than if simply a passive note-taker, and there is a real value to the smallness of the group. Tutorials of this kind are also excellent preparation for classes which require active participation by at least most of those present to be effective.

So are tutorials useful? In short the 'bad' version described above is (as a tutorial) close to useless, except in so far as it means that unmotivated students are more likely to pass than fail, but the 'good' version has some impressive and arguably unique features. It is an opportunity for difficult parts of the core material to be sorted out in a highly focused way, without wasting time on things that the student already understands, and an opportunity for quite intense discussion and questioning (by both sides) which is a key route towards deep understanding as well as the ideal of "Thanks, you taught me how to think".

Before moving on it may be of interest to reflect on whether tutorials in economics may differ much from those in other subjects, either in format or in usefulness relative to lectures, etc. The honest answer to the first of these is that I have no idea (I'm looking forward to reading the other chapters in this book!), but my guess is that there may be some difference, if only at the margin, in two respects. Firstly, understanding economics is very much a cumulative process both across different areas of the subject and over time as the material becomes more complex. Hence there are sizeable knock-on benefits from getting core, early material well sorted out, or put another way there are very large costs to someone losing touch with the subject and staying that way as would be more likely in a less personalised teaching system. Secondly, while the best tutorials occasionally approach the ideal of a 'dialogue of equals', it is problematic if the tutor is not well up to speed on the nitty-gritty of a topic. Someone with a well-trained economist's mind will usually be very good at 'big picture' discussions, and certainly good at asking awkward questions that will provoke thought, but, unless the tutor can focus tightly on technical details or queries as they arise, such discussions will often become sloppy. In my view these points imply that tutorials may be especially beneficial in economics but they require some specialisation on the tutor's side; success requires a lot more than just two or three bright people in a room with a topic to discuss.

The above has addressed the intellectual dimension to economics tutorials but there are at least three others: work incentives; learning more broadly defined rather than just learning economics; and self-confidence and mindset issues. I shall be brief on these since they are not specific to economics tutorials though I believe that each is important in an economics context. On incentives there are both negative and positive points to be made. The negative one is simply that tutorials are compulsory and the smallness of the group ("There's nowhere to hide") means that students will usually want to avoid the embarrassment of being obviously at sea with the topic. The positive point is that for a thoughtful student, tutorials are an almost unique opportunity to have queries answered, raise questions more broadly and develop their own views with a well-informed and critical (but hopefully encouraging) debating partner, all of which should be a strong incentive to think about the material in advance.

What about learning in general? The 'bad' tutorial has little value for 'learning how to learn', let alone 'learning how to think' or acquiring other skills – more a matter of 'learning how to get away with it' – but the 'good' tutorial is seriously different. For a thoughtful and motivated student the tutorial system can be an excellent vehicle for picking up learning and general professional skills; concentration during passive learning beforehand (staying awake in lectures...), research skills when going through a reading list ("Is what I'm reading really relevant, have I read enough to have a good crack at the essay question?"), analytical skills ("What are the key points, what's the answer?"), critical skills ("These authors think they know the answer but do they?"), writing skills in preparing essays, and verbal discussion and 'thinking on one's feet' skills in the tutorial itself. All of these should be reinforced over time if tutorials include helpful feedback, and the rapid frequency of tutorials and that feedback mean lots of practice. The educational experts would no doubt present a more polished list, but to my mind that is an impressive set of capabilities for later professional life. Perhaps the one important omission is presentation skills, but these are anyway often practised in small group classes.

Lastly, and perhaps most importantly, tutorials are likely to impact strongly on students' self-confidence and general approach to their work. Effective learning requires not just motivation ("I want to do this"), but also self-confidence ("I *can* do this"): though without over-confidence ("I can do this easily so there's no need to think much"). At Oxford we are privileged to teach many very gifted people but it is common for students to feel that they are less able than they are (often a majority of a year-group feel initially that they just about scraped in at admissions and that everyone else will be much brighter than them...), though the opposite can occur too. Obviously an unsympathetic tutor can make this much worse but, all being well, tutorials should offer excellent opportunities for feedback that is positive (while always being honest), and the frequency of feedback should help the process whereby students settle in mentally and feel that, subject to the required effort, they can be successful.

So what does it all add up to? If much of the above sounds like a hard-sell on tutorial teaching may I simply re-state that none of the benefits of tutorials are automatic. Lots can go wrong, and, if it does, there is little that tutorials can offer beyond what would happen in a lecture plus large classes system. But the upside potential is huge if tutors and students pull their weight.

What else should one say to the student reader? I hope the above is a useful glimpse into the tutor's mindset and a source of some suggestions on how to make the most of the system. The message is not just work hard (because everyone says that) but that tutors will respond well if you do fully participate: and there are some sizeable hidden costs to not doing so (unmotivated tutor, one-sided tutorials with little time for the more interesting material). None of this means that you have to be a future Nobel prizewinner to profit from tutorials; just that you engage with the process in a pro-active way. Start from wherever you are and aim to move on. Your tutors are very unlikely ever to be your examiners (and if they are it's anonymous), so there is no need to hesitate in asking questions across the whole spectrum from the finer points to something on page one of the textbook (which can sometimes be more funda-mental anyway). On the practical side, aim to arrive at a tutorial with a list of points that you want clarified or things that you would like to discuss and ask for frank feedback if you feel that you are not receiving enough pointers on how well you are doing and whether you are approaching things effectively.

On the wider issue of the usefulness of tutorials and their future, I have tried to argue that successful tutorials have very significant benefits throughout the course which would be lost if they disappeared; that they are fully modern in nature; and that they work best in tandem with (and not as a substitute for) other formats such as lectures and classes. If we did not have them already they would need to be invented. I do hope that we can go on affording them.

11. The History Tutorial: 'You have taught yourself this term'
Christopher Tyerman, Fellow in History, Hertford College, Oxford

This possibly double-edged comment, delivered to me by one of my tutors during my first year as an undergraduate, signals the difference of the tutorial system to other forms of academic instruction. However it was meant by the somewhat awkward and testy don, I took it as a compliment. Having now giving perhaps over 5,000 tutorials myself, the comment seems rather neatly to sum up what the tutorial method is all about. A tutorial is not a lesson, although information is often imparted. It is not a lecture, although some tutors (and at times I would have to plead guilty to this) develop verbal compulsive didacticism syndrome. It is not a seminar, although especially if more than one undergraduate is present or a text is being studied, the tone can be similar. As each tutorial encounter is by definition different and individual, generalisations tend to the banal, the trite and the obvious. What makes tutorials (good and bad) distinctive as a way of academic exchange is that they are unavoidably shared occasions, social as well as academic events. This can be daunting to the tyro student, but it is the essence of the exercise. The pupil enters the space of the tutor who is forced to interact with the student who, in a sense, becomes a guest. Even in the most old-fashioned and formal of such meetings, tutor and pupil are literally on a level, usually sitting facing each other. This physical egalitarianism is conducive to intellectual sharing, even if it does not necessarily preclude academic posturing (by both parties). As most tutorials occur in the tutor's own room, in college or department, even the most astringent tutor is in a potentially vulnerable position as the student's eye wanders over the bookshelves, the décor, the pictures (if any), the furnishings, the mess (or lack of it). All of this unavoidably reveals something of the personality of the tutor. None of the participants in a tutorial have a place to hide. This can be frightening for those new to the system. However, it does ensure that, willy-nilly, some sort of contact is established. While the worst sort of tutorial style is that of forced *bonhomie* (from either party), the social and the academic merge naturally and inextricably. According to another of my old tutors, a necessary ingredient of a memorable tutorial is for the student to be given something; it could be an idea, an interpretation, an argument, a fact, a joke, a biscuit, a cup of coffee, a drink....

Each academic discipline has it own take on the nature and role of tutorials. The study of History presents its own particular difficulties, whether pursued through tutorials or any other sort of exercise. In some ways, the idea of 'teaching History' is a misnomer. Information on personally or institutionally selected topics can be imparted in any variety of methods, but the engagement, understanding or empathetic response tends to be experienced rather than imparted. At every stage, the process of assimilating knowledge and making sense of it requires a personal imaginative contact with the past. Many people simply do not 'get 'History'. Enthusiasm can be inspired by teachers, but largely through force of personality or their own excitement with the subject that conveys their sense of its importance to others. Interest in History comes from inside, by practice and by example.

Tutorials are an obvious forum for this alchemy. Yet, in fact, the procedure is far from mysterious. The essence of most History tutorials is the weekly essay, written on the basis of books and articles suggested the week before by the tutor but often without much other direction. The essay provides the undergraduate's prime contribution to the tutorial; it sets the initial direction, terms of engagement, and, in most cases, the launching point for discussion. In this way, the pupil can shape the tutorial as much as the tutor. However, the tutorial is not a place to report on the week's work, rather it is an opportunity to discuss problems raised by the reading set and the essay written before excursions into wider, often highly tangential subjects connected with the set topic. This exploration of a previously probably unfamiliar topic is conducted by this dual verbal process, literary and oral. In this it mimics much of professional life of the sort that most History undergraduates find themselves involved in after leaving Oxford: mastering a brief in a short time; writing a brief assessment of the main problems and possible solutions; and discussing and defending the opinions expressed in meetings. I think these are called life skills, and find application from business to law, banking to teaching, accountancy to administration or in the civil service.

There are more specific aspects of the tutorial that suit the exploration of History. At the heart of the tutorial, it purpose and procedure, lie discussion, debate and challenge. These are also the fundamentals of historical investigation. The first things all History undergraduates have to be weaned off are the certainties derived from confidently prescriptive A-Level courses. They soon learn that no primary source, influential monograph or famous text book, no interpretations and arguments- even, perhaps especially, those of the tutor- are immune from attack and testing. That is why History is such a good general arts education as well as a good preparation for mature scholarship. Historians are a quarrelsome, some might suggest querulous lot. It is in the nature of the discipline to contest orthodoxy, to be suspicious of accepted wisdom, and this is in general a salutary way of regarding the world. For historians, by itself the surviving evidence from the past is inert. One of its greatest myths is that History is simply a list of uncontested facts. Evidence only comes alive and makes any sense when selected, analysed, organised and interpreted. This cannot be a neutral or entirely value free activity. Historians will inevitably disagree. From that disagreement comes deeper understanding- and deeper disagreement. The tutorial is based on discussion, testing ideas and posing counter arguments, the historical method in genteel – or sometimes not so genteel – miniature. This questioning, occasionally seemingly aggressive, at times, it might appear to the outsider, destructive technique, is often the hardest aspect for new undergraduates to appreciate. It can descend into sustained negativity; but it can also provide the basis for constructing each undergraduate's confidence in their own ideas and opinions, which is what the whole exercise is all about; not knowledge but thought, and sustained critical thought at that. As was said of one of the great and somewhat rebarbative forensic History dons of the mid-twentieth century, 'he always went for the ball not the man', often appending 'sorry' to some devastating assault on the undergraduate's lack of evidence in support of some claim or other. Given the fashion for mollycoddling of the young, such techniques can be rather bracing when first encountered. Equally, however, the tutorial system is sensitive to less robust souls who need to be quietly brought out of themselves and given confidence to embark on criticisms of their own. This is why the one to one or one to two model is so important. The brash and the bully can be brash, bullying and bullied. But the meek can also inherit the earth.

The reputation of the tutorial system is both sustained and wrecked by anecdotes, many *ben trovato*; many true. What both fact and fiction expose is why outside planners dislike it. The effectiveness of any tutorial relies on the personalities of those involved (student as well as tutor), not on some grid of assessed targets and teaching criteria. This makes for an uneven system, unpredictable and varied. Rather like life itself. One frequent complaint levelled by first-year undergraduates is that many tutors refuse to give precise marks to tutorial essays, inadequate 'feedback' as it called. As most students have spent all their conscious life being graded and assessed this absence produces a form of withdrawal anxiety. Yet the gap between school and university approaches to learning is the point. The tutorial system pits the student against his or herself, not some Great Mark Scheme In The Sky. Every undergraduate who has produced a feeble effort based on a brief encounter with a text book and some caffeine-fuelled hours lit by the midnight oil will know as well as, if not better than their tutor how wretched the result can be, and how far below their potential. In this prolonged investigation into self-knowledge and self-awareness which constitutes university life, the tutor is a companion not a judge, critical maybe, forbidding occasionally, but, provided the pupil is not a recidivist slacker, usually supportive. Given that Oxford dons, because of the intensive personal tutorial system, teach more hours than almost any other academics in similar universities across the world, why else would they bother?

There are as many ways to give a good tutorial as there are good tutors; there are as many ways to waste a tutorial as there are unengaged undergraduates. There is an unspoken contract between pupil and tutor. The concentrated nature of the Oxford terms, with their emphasis on students working by and for themselves for most of the time, places responsibility on the undergraduate. But it also means s/he can make of the course what s/he wants. Then tutor is there to help, to guide and to prod, but mainly to witness. In that shared responsibility lies the system's strength. Pupils learn things in tutorials, about the subject, about their tutors, about themselves. But tutors learn as well, a fact often greeted with incredulity by their students. Many of the most productive publishing Oxford historians have been the most engaged and prolific tutors. The link is no accident. Intellectual exchange is not necessarily about showing off superior weight of information. The tutorial system lacks system. Instead it has method, one mind trying to help others to find their own way and their own voice. History, like all other subjects, cannot be done properly by automatons, only by individuals, undergraduates as well as dons. This inevitably allows, insists on even, the play of eccentricity, omission, diversity, difference. Without the personal, learning might as well become an online download. There are many ways of doing History, teaching it and learning it. However, the tutorial remains one of the best, most efficient and effective ways of encouraging the necessary individual critical approach to ideas and arguments because it reflects and encourages precisely what education is actually about, granting and gaining not knowledge but independence.

12. The Oxford Tutorial in the Context of Theory on Student Learning: "Knowledge is a wild thing, and must be hunted before it can be tamed"

Suzanne Shale, sometime Director, Institute for the Advancement of University Learning, University of Oxford, and sometime Fellow in Law, New College

At Oxford in my youth the Senior Tutor's formula in reporting on my work to the Head of the College would never be: "Mr. Moore is being taught by Dr. X." It would be: "Mr. Moore is reading this part of his subject with Dr. X." I have come to see that two worlds lie within these expressions. (W.G. Moore)

It [higher education] educates the intellect to reason well in all matters, to reach out towards truth, and to grasp it". (J. H. Newman)

What is the purpose of an Oxford tutorial? And how does it work? In some respects the only possible answer to those questions is: "it all depends…"

It depends upon the views of the tutors and students who find themselves working together. For what each expects of the tutorial, wants of the tutorial, and is prepared to bring to the tutorial, will shape its purpose. Equally though, it depends upon shared cultures of learning. Tutors and students derive their expectations of tutorials, their intentions for tutorials, and their views on what each should contribute to them, from the educational culture of their times.

All of the essays in this collection reflect the individual perspectives of tutors and students working in Oxford today. But those perspectives inevitably draw upon deeper assumptions about the nature of higher education, and about how we engage in higher learning. This essay considers the question of what higher learning is, how according to higher education research it happens, and what the Oxford tutorial might contribute to the learning of students engaged in it.

A consensus on higher learning

Many academics – who would agree about little else – do seem to agree about what comprises higher learning. Higher learning demands that students do more than learn to reproduce information. Instead they are called upon to master, transform and create knowledge. Early in the twentieth century A.N. Whitehead wrote an influential essay in which he argued that:

> The university imparts information, but it imparts it imaginatively… This atmosphere of excitement, arising from imaginative consideration, transforms knowledge. A fact is no longer a bare fact: it is invested with all its possibilities. It is no longer a burden on the memory: it is energising as the poet of our dreams, and as the architect of our purposes.

The now defunct Council for National Academic Awards (CNAA) used to describe the aims of higher education in similar if rather less lyrical terms. They wrote that higher education courses should foster:

> the development of students' intellectual and imaginative powers; their understanding and judgement; their problem-solving skills; their ability to communicate; their ability to see relationships within what they have learned and to perceive their field of study in a broader perspective. [They] must aim to stimulate an enquiring, analytical and creative approach, encouraging independent judgement and critical self-awareness.

Is contemporary higher education truly such a creative affair? It is often said of the sciences, in particular, that there is a great deal of factual material that students must learn in their undergraduate years before they can move into the more contested (and interesting?) areas of their subject. But, while it may be true that there is factual material to be *learned*, it is not true that the factual material merely has to be memorised. All academics expect their students to be able to do more than recite random facts. They want them to be able to apply their knowledge to novel problems, to understand the weight and status of different principles, to appreciate the limits of their current understanding. This requires a creative, inquiring attitude of mind. If they are to be able to use what they learn for their own ends, one way or another students must convert newly presented information into their own flexible knowledge.

Higher learning is a process of questioning many of the ideas and beliefs that are otherwise taken for granted. That is how new knowledge is created. So universities inevitably and ineluctably challenge the *status quo*, whether that is the *status quo* of science, the arts, politics, or culture, and whether that is the *status quo* of influential groups or the *status quo* of individual beliefs. Professor Ronald Barnett writes that:

> A genuine higher learning is subversive in the sense of subverting the student's taken-for-granted world, including the world of endeavour, scholarship, calculation or creativity, into which he or she has been initiated. A genuine higher education is unsettling; it is not meant to be a cosy experience. It is disturbing because, ultimately, the student comes to see that things could always be other than they are. A higher education experience is not complete unless the student realizes that, no matter how much effort is put in, or how much library research, there are no final answers.

If tutorials have an overriding purpose, then that purpose must be to promote the creative, transformative, and even subversive nature of higher learning. To understand how tutorials might do this, we need to know a little more about how students learn.

Student approaches to higher learning
Over one hundred years of research into learning have generated many different accounts of how students learn. In this brief essay, I shall focus on just one of them.

In the past quarter of a century the idea that students adopt either 'deep' or 'surface' approaches to study has become one of the most influential ways of explaining how students learn in higher education. It all started in 1976, with the publication of a study conducted by two Swedish researchers. They discovered that students who were asked to read an academic article, and afterwards answer questions on it, approached the task in two very different ways.

They found that some students perceived the text as an assemblage of separate items of information that should be memorised in order to answer the anticipated questions. The researchers called this a 'surface approach'. Other students treated the text as something that contained a structure of meaning. They searched for its underlying concerns, its implications, and its meaning to themselves. This, the researchers called the 'deep approach'. Students who approached the task using a deep approach understood more of the article, were better able to answer a range of questions about it, and were also able to remember it more effectively.

A great deal of subsequent research demonstrated that these different approaches to learning emerge across a wide range of academic tasks. Research has also shown that students may be quite strategic in their approaches to study, and use these deep or surface approaches within a strategic context.

Promoting deep approaches to learning
The research into deep and surface approaches to learning is of real importance, because in these two approaches we see encapsulated our aspirations for undergraduate scholarship. The dull transfer of data from one human machine to another could in principle be accomplished using surface approaches. But the exhilarating development of human capacities that I wrote of earlier in this essay clearly demands something more.

Deep and surface approaches to learning are not personality traits. Research has demonstrated that the very same students can, and do, adopt a deep approach or a surface approach at different times and in response to different tasks. So what encourages students to adopt deep or surface approaches to learning?

The answer seems to lie in a combination of *what it is that students are asked to do* (and therefore the demands that are *actually* being placed upon them) and *students' perceptions of what it is that they are being asked to do* (and therefore what they *believe* the demands are). What tutors expect students to do in preparation for tutorials, and what students are expected to do in the tutorial itself, are, therefore, important matters. But equally important is what students *perceive* to be the purposes of tutorial preparation and the tutorial itself.

Tutors rarely use the terminology of deep and surface approaches to learning, but they do tend to describe tutorials in ways that indicate they use them to encourage deep approaches. So what is known about how students use tutorials? The answer is, not enough! Oxford is currently carrying out research into this question, but in the meantime existing studies can get us some way towards understanding how students experience tutorials. This research is discussed in the next section.

Conceptions of learning

Research suggests that adult learners conceive of learning in six significantly different ways, as set out below. These different ways operate as a 'nested hierarchy'. This means that someone who holds conception 6 may also express conception 1 in appropriate contexts, but that someone who holds conception 1 will not express, and may not understand, conception 6.

- *Conception 1: Increasing the quantity of information of which the individual is aware*

- *Conception 2: Memorising*

- *Conception 3: The acquisition of facts, methods, and techniques which can be retained and used when necessary*

- *Conception 4: The abstraction of meaning*

- *Conception 5: An interpretative process aimed at understanding reality*

- *Conception 6: Learning as about changing as a person*

The first three conceptions of learning correlate with surface approaches to study. Students who believe that learning is about the absorption of facts, is about memorisation, or is about mastering techniques, will tend to adopt a surface approach to study. The latter three conceptions of learning correlate with deep approaches to study. Students who believe that learning is about the creation of new structures of meaning, or about developing ways of interpreting reality, or about changing as a person, will be more likely to adopt a deep approach.

So what happens when students holding these different conceptions of learning encounter the tutorial system? The research suggests that they will treat tutorials in a way that is consistent with their current conception of learning. If a student thinks that learning is the mastery of techniques, he or she will think that the purpose of a tutorial is to teach techniques. If a student thinks that learning is an interpretative process aimed at understanding reality, he or she will treat tutorials as a place in which to explore different frameworks for understanding reality.

The astute reader will have noticed that there is some considerable scope for confusion here. We would expect tutors to hold the higher conceptions of learning. But first year students in particular may continue to hold some of the lower ones. Tutors and students may meet in tutorials in possession of quite discrepant conceptions of learning. They may, therefore, find their views on what tutorials are for to be quite at odds – at least for a time.

What can tutorials achieve?

Although they may start out with different conceptions of learning, tutors and students do not pass each other like proverbial ships in the night. One of the great strengths of the tutorial system is that it enables tutors and students to engage in a dialogue that demands more sophisticated levels of understanding, and suggests new conceptions of learning. Tutorial teaching encourages students to make the discovery that higher learning is different from, and demands more of them, than learning as they may previously have conceived of it.

It is something of this sort, perhaps, that W.G. Moore had in mind when he wrote of the two worlds that lay within the expressions, "Mr. Moore is being taught by Dr. X." and "Mr. Moore is reading this part of his subject with Dr. X." 'Being taught by Dr. X' suggests a world in which students and their learning are the objects of other people's – that is tutors' – endeavours. On the other hand, a student 'reading this part of her subject with Dr. X.' is engaged in a working partnership in which her own endeavours lie at the heart of her learning and are really of far greater significance than the efforts of her tutors.

Not only does this latter view of things more closely accord with the world of the tutorial as the Oxford tutor sees it, but it more closely accords with the working week as the Oxford student will experience it. For each tutorial hour spent working with a tutor, a student will probably have worked at least another nineteen hours alone. (Some students will have worked many more hours than this, and others undoubtedly less, but, whatever the actual figure, the tutorial hour represents only a very small part of the time that students spend learning.) The tutorial's importance, then, lies in what it prompts students to do when they are working alone, as much as in what happens when students and tutors are working together.

To pursue our shipping metaphor, the tutorial is not the journey itself. It is the means by which students may chart their course. So, although tutorials may occupy only a small part of students' time, as guides to the navigation of deep waters they are not unimportant.

In a paper published in 1989, Chickering and Gamson summarised the implications of some fifty years of American research into higher learning. Among the seven fundamental principles of good undergraduate teaching that they identified were four strongly interpersonal factors: personal contact between students and tutors; the communication of high expectations; respect for diverse talents and approaches to learning; and developing co-operation between students. The first three of these have long been thought to be an integral part of the Oxford Tutorial with its intense individual focus in the weekly hour. Concomitantly, co-operation between students has sometimes been thought of as the tutorial's weakness. In fact, students appear to co-operate quite actively outside of the tutorial, building informal alliances as a means of coping with its demands.

I suggested earlier that a higher education worthy of its name must have a subversive element, that it inevitably questions the *status quo*. 'Subversive' may seem an odd description of many higher education institutions, which to those outside can often appear bastions of establishment conservatism. But curiously, even in Oxford, subversion is at work. A sceptical, inquiring stance lies right at the very heart of tutorial teaching. No beliefs are unquestionable, no statement is safe from scrutiny, no evidence is incontrovertible, and no conclusion is inescapable.

Even your tutor's.

i   W.G. Moore *The Tutorial System and its Future* (Oxford: Pergamon Press, 1968) p.20

ii   J.H. Newman ii *The Idea of a University* (1852; 1873 edition) p. 95

iii A.N. Whitehead 'Universities and their function' in *The Aims of Education and Other Essays*. (New York: Free Press, 1967), cited in P. Ramsden *Learning to Teach in Higher Education* (London: Routledge, 1992) p. 19

iv   R. Barnett *The Idea of Higher Education* (Buckingham: Open University Press, 1990) p. 155*British Journal of Educational Psychology* 46, pp. 4-11

v   F. Marton and R. Säljö 'On qualitative differences in learning. 1 – Outcome and Process' *British Journal of Educational Psychology* 46, pp 4-11

iii N.J. Entwistle *The Impact of Teaching on Learning Outcomes in Higher Education – A Literature Review* (Sheffield: CVCP, 1992) p 12; citing N.J. Entwistle 'Student learning and study strategies' in B.R. Clark and G. Neave (eds) *The Encyclopedia of Higher Education* (Oxford: Pergamon Press, 1992)

vii R. Säljö *Learning in the Learner's Perspective, 1* – Some Commonsense Conceptions Reports from the Institute of Education, University of Gothenburg, No 77 (1979), cited in E. Martin and P. Ramsden 'Learning Skills or Skill in Learning' in *Student Learning-Research in Education and Cognitive Psychology* eds. J.T.E. Richardson, Michael W. Eysenck and D. Warren Piper (Buckingham: Open University Press, 1987) pp 155-167

viii A.W. Chickering and Z.F. Gamson *Seven Principles for Good Practice in Undergraduate Education* (Racine, Wisc: Johnson Foundation, 1989)

13. Been there; Got the T-shirt: The perspective of a recent survivor of the tutorial system...

Andrew Smith, sometime Weston Junior Research Fellow in Chemistry, New College

I started Oxford as an undergraduate (Jesus College, 1992) and have been through the whole of the tutorial system. Having received the benefits of such tuition, to now being on the giving side as a tutor, I hope to be able to lend my experience of the system, with the aim of giving some insight into what leads to a successful partnership between tutor and undergraduate.

As a first year undergraduate I can recollect being given my first tutorial piece in a brisk meeting at the start of 0th week. After a brief welcome from my tutors, it was straight down to business, with a complete breakdown of the planned year's work leading up to prelims in the summer. The differences between a 'tutorial' and a 'class' were described and tutorial pairings distributed. It was made clear that the emphasis of the work would be directed through problem solving to developing the skills required to think as a chemist, with the initiative and emphasis placed squarely on my shoulders. My tutors would be there to advise and probe, not to simply deliver information as I had previously been used to. Like most of the other undergraduates in the room I had worked hard toward the 'A' levels I had needed to gain my place at Oxford, but had the knowledge and confidence that my grades were always going to be under control. This was now a very different environment. In a room full of talented people I no longer knew what was expected, would no longer be told exactly what to do. It seemed that I would have to develop my own feeling for the subject, my own understanding as opposed to relying upon facts for comfort.

I remember being worried, and rightly so as my first tutorial piece was a disaster – I felt hopelessly out of my depth. In my first group class I remember feeling naïve as my fellow tutees were quickly discussing topics they had covered at school that I had not encountered. I was too embarrassed, felt too uncomfortable to ask the questions that I needed answering so that I could find my own starting point for the work. I didn't want to be behind the rest of the group. I felt out of place and, more importantly, out of my depth.

Luckily, I was given a fantastic piece of advice: "Who cares?"... Who cares if you ask what to others may seem an obvious question? Who cares what your fellow tutees think about what you find difficult? Who cares if you attempt a question and get it wrong? I had to realise that tutorials were there for my benefit and in this way soon learnt the most valuable tool of the tutorial system. As an undergraduate you need to be able to acquire the information that you need to proceed; this process is most efficient if a two-way understanding between tutor and tutee is reached. Firstly, participation from the tutee is a prerequisite. You need to cover the work that you are set, you need to give feedback to the tutor as to which topics you find most difficult, and you must be able to contribute in class discussions. The tutor will try and encourage you to think for yourself, and be able to readily define the boundaries between telling you the answer and giving you just enough information so that you can figure out the answers, and a way of tackling various problems for yourself.

So don't be afraid to get things wrong... I think that I managed to make what some people would call a 'fool' of myself in many tutorials, when I decided to attempt something that I thought I knew the answer to but my logic was flawed. Yet in doing so, I was readily able to learn and I felt part of the system, as opposed to being alienated from it, and so gained in confidence. Once the fear of being incorrect has vanished, tutorials will become more probing, more interesting, even enjoyable... From my own undergraduate perspective, that is the most important lesson that I picked up at an early stage. Do not be put off or over-awed; you need to find what you want from the tutorial system. It will be there and the tutors are there to help you find what you are looking for.

Having completed my undergraduate degree, I began teaching as a first year D.Phil student. I asked myself "What makes a good tutor?" As an undergraduate I had several fantastic tutors who managed to readily pass on their enthusiasm and knowledge for chemistry. They were able to give their own interpretation to the subject, their own perspective, with their own particular character. You cannot, therefore, expect your various tutors to approach tutorials in the same way. That would take the variety from the tuition system here in Oxford, and detract from the learning experience. They will each impress something of their own character upon you, their own methods, their own way of thinking, gently trying to mould you, trying to introduce you to the tools, the questions that you need to be able to ask yourself to be able to succeed. That is what the whole of the Oxford tutorial system relies upon and what makes it distinct and special. From my own experience, I believe that the best way to teach is to be able to break the most complicated problems down into small, manageable chunks of information, which, when put together, make sense. Others may disagree; but by seeing a range of approaches you can start to think for yourself which is a necessity for success. Your tutors are there only as guides; they cannot tell you the answers to every single question you will need for Prelims or Finals, although they can encourage you along the right lines.

What immediately struck me about tutorials from a teaching perspective is how quickly you can tell those students who have fully attempted the work and those that have copied the work. How readily you can distinguish between those struggling with the workload but trying hard, and those that are coasting and trying to bluff their way through. Those that are enthusiastic, and those going through the motions. You have to give your tutors some credit as most of them have been through the same or similar systems, and seen (even done?) most of the tricks themselves. So don't kid yourself into thinking that you managed to get away with it, because you are only letting yourself down. It is far too easy to blame your tutors for any of your own downfalls; the tutorial system is there to encourage you to find your own goals and decide for yourself where you want to go – and then to give you the opportunity to achieve them and to get there. Coming to Oxford gives you an opportunity to do so many different things, but if you miss out on the full benefit of the tutorial system you will not fulfil your potential and have only yourself to blame.

So what can you expect in a tutorial? Speaking as a chemist, tutorials for science-based subjects will typically be centred around problem-solving as opposed to essay-writing, although that is not to say that you will never have to write essays! Do not be surprised if you find yourself in a class for which you have prepared and handed in written work only to find yourself then hauled up to a white board to answer questions without your notes. One of the best ways of actually understanding your subject is to be forced to attempt to tackle problems from first principles when you don't immediately know the answer. There is no simple substitute for getting up to the board in front of your friends, forgetting what you've worked on for the last week, and still managing to work your way through the problem to the answer. In that way you are tested upon not only your knowledge, but you will simultaneously be encouraged to develop your own rules and strategies. As tutorials are broadly problem-based, you cannot rely upon a tutorial partner to give all the answers, nor to read out their essay for that particular week while you relax a little. Science problems allow each person in a class to be readily tested, as the tutorial is easily broken down into distinct sections. Never forget that tutorials are designed not only to cover the basic, core knowledge necessary for the subject, but also to stretch even the best students to the limit. Tutorials cannot, however, teach you everything that you need to know. They are an aid to your degree studies and are meant to compliment, rather than replace lectures. All you have to do is make the most of them!

14. The Oxford Tutorial from the Students' Perspective

James Clark, sometime Fellow in Modern History, Brasenose College

Like the admissions interview itself, there is no shortage of stories about what it is like to have a tutorial at Oxford, but a truly accurate account is much harder to come by. Certainly, there is little or no enlightenment to be found amongst the celebrated authorities on Oxford life. Charles Dodgson (Lewis Carroll) claimed that the principal purpose of the tutorial was for 'the tutor to be dignified and to remain at a distance from his pupil' – he thought, preferably in a different room – 'and for the pupil to be degraded'. Evelyn Waugh, who with his 'poor third' presumably could claim only a passing acquaintance with tutorial teaching, considered there was little to be gained from close confinement with tutors 'who give the impression of having been suddenly stirred from a deep, eternal slumber [in his case with] the untimely mention of Wales'. Even in our own day, we still trade tales of the best, worst and wackiest in teaching experiences. There is any number of eccentric dons; the tutor who gets up and leaves the room when the student has barely begun his essay; the tutor who falls sound asleep; the tutor who insists on listening to essays whilst lying prone on the floor. There are also the undergraduates behaving badly; the student who comes to tutorials in pajamas, clutching a cup of tea; the student who reads a perfect, precise essay, from a blank sheet of paper; the student who is bad – or brave – enough to plagiarize from one of his own tutor's books.

Of course, a genuine insight into tutorial teaching can only really be gained from speaking to those students who are currently studying in Oxford, before distance, dementia or the desire for revenge has distorted their views. To this end over the past academic year (1999/2000), I interviewed no fewer than forty undergraduates to find out what they thought about the tutorials they had experienced. They were drawn from six different colleges – roughly a fifth of the total number – and from a variety of arts and science subjects. There was a mix of first-, second-, third- and fourth-year students, and a little over half of the interviewees were women. Their response was enthusiastic: tutorials continue to play a prominent part in the life of any student at Oxford and there is no doubt that they think about them a great deal, how they work (and sometimes do not work) as a way of learning and teaching. Their views should be of interest to both critics and supporters of the system.

In the first place, it is very clear from the students' comments that there is much about tutorial teaching that has changed, and continues to change in contemporary Oxford. For the most part, of course, the tutorial does still set the pattern for the students' week; it is still their principal point-of-contact with their tutors and the focus of most (if not all) of their written assignments. Generally speaking it is also still a college-based activity, allowing students to form a close relationship with others of their cohort in the same subject area. But in other respects it has become something very different. The traditional one-on-one tutorial, between a tutor and a single student who reads an essay – or presents some other assignment – and receives (often peremptory) feedback is undoubtedly a thing of the past. It is now very common for students to take a course of tutorials in pairs, and many of those interviewed had also experienced them in groups of three or four. In the Sciences groups can be larger still. This seems to have been a welcome change. Most agree that there is far more to be gained from group discussion than from the somewhat stilted exchanges between a tutor and a single student. Generally, these larger tutorials have allowed a less formal and more natural atmosphere to develop in which students find it easier to express their views.

In many cases, the role of the essay (or other written assignment) in the tutorial has also changed. In many of the arts subjects it is now common for students to submit their written work prior to the tutorial, so whilst it does still form the basis of the discussion there is no time lost to a formal reading. In groups of three or four, it is often the case that the tutor will invite each student to give a brief presentation of their views on the subject as they have emerged in the preparation of the essay, before opening up the tutorial to a wider discussion. Once again, most students see this as a change for the better. Reading aloud has long been unpopular, both on practical – it uses up valuable time – and pedagogic grounds, tending as it does to reinforce the division between themselves and the tutor. In a less formally structured setting where no assignment is read in its entirety, students say they have found the confidence to enter fully into discussion with their tutors, to challenge interpretations and test out ideas of their own. Perhaps the only problem from the students' point of view is that it is now difficult to find an opportunity to discuss the specific strengths and weaknesses of their own written work. There is a danger that with the decline of one-on-one teaching we lose the opportunity to offer the kind of detailed, in-depth advice to an individual that was always a distinctive feature of the traditional tutorial.

Of course, the inner workings of a tutorial are not always (if ever) familiar to students when they first come up to Oxford. [Hence this book! – Editor.] Many admitted that they had arrived with the image of an arrogant, authoritarian tutor whose only aim was to expose the intellectual weakness of his students. Some said they had benefited from the Student Survival Kit and other similar advice booklets issued by a number of colleges, which try to de-bunk some of the more pervasive myths about student life. There are not yet enough of these manuals, however, to counteract some of the more disturbing impressions conveyed in the media and colluded in by the more mischievous alumni. New students remain nervous about speaking in front of their tutor, expecting the tutorial to be something similar to their original interview. They are also uncomfortable about confronting an acknowledged expert in their field, fearing they will find themselves out of their depth. There is also a suspicion that the tutorial does serve as one, unspoken mode of assessment, even if a written assignment is not given a formal mark. For many though the greatest anxiety is quite simply not to know exactly what it is that their tutor expects from them in each tutorial. Most of the students I spoke to said that their understanding of tutorials had grown only slowly, largely through a process of trial and error. Like many aspects of Oxford life, it seems that many tutors themselves still regard the art of the tutorial as something that cannot be taught and that understanding comes only through some mystical process of self-realization. Some tutors – especially the younger generation of college fellows – do now give their students guidance on how to approach and how to make the most of their tutorials. But it seems in most cases it is only after two or three terms, and sometimes after Mods or Prelims, that students say they are entirely sure about what they expect to do in, and take away from, their tutorials.

Once they have mastered the art, there is no doubt that most of the students do find their tutorials to be a great source of stimulation. Many draw a contrast with their experiences at school where direct access to tutors was limited and where class sizes and timetable demands meant the syllabus was covered only superficially and at a break-neck pace. Those I interviewed especially appreciated the degree of focus possible in a tutorial setting, where the finer points of a subject, its factual content but also its further implications could be painstakingly picked apart. At the same time, students also enthuse about the breadth of discussion possible in their tutorials. In comparison to lectures, or seminars that they often find contrived, in their weekly exchanges with their tutor and one or more partner they found there is far greater scope to explore a wide range of themes. There is a marked preference for those tutors who do not set any very specific agenda for discussion, and when spur-of-the-moment ideas can be pursued to their logical conclusion. Some liked it best if the tutorial became a testing-ground for ideas, an opportunity to identify problems and raise questions. Others preferred there to be a conscious debate over one, or a cluster of issues. If these discussions become heated then so much the better from the students' point of view; as one of them put it, 'the best tutorials are like Newsnight with the tutor as Paxman'. Either way, it is agreed that the advantage of the tutorial when it is working like this is that discussion is open, and open-ended, and there is every opportunity for the students to chose the direction or focus of it for themselves.

It would be wrong, of course, to claim that current students' opinions of tutorial teaching are unwaveringly positive. Most maintain that the character and quality of tutorials varies enormously across the University, and that much may depend on a chance meeting with a charismatic tutor in a single term. There was a suspicion – in this author's opinion, unfounded – that there is more to be gained from a tutorial led by a graduate student or a younger tutor than from a more mature, established scholar. Perhaps a more convincing point is that the great strength of the tutorial, that is to say the opportunity it provides for interaction between tutor and student on a personal level, can also on occasion serve as its greatest weakness. It does demand that the student can establish a good (and good-natured) working relationship with their tutor and, for a variety of reasons as much to do with the student as with tutor themselves, this is not always the case. Some students also made the more specific criticism that, whilst tutorials are an important forum for debate and discussion, they are poor preparation for the examinations (whether Mods, Prelims or Schools) themselves. In their view tutorials do nothing to expand their knowledge of their subject and yet it is this subject knowledge that forms the basis of the examinations. One interviewee opined: 'tutorials have taught me to argue…about anything, but not how to pass the exam'.

A small minority of students also raised a further point of criticism; that the tutorial system as practiced at Oxford is inherently gendered, favouring styles of learning that are more natural to men than to women. In their view the emphasis on debate and discussion in a tutorial setting places male students at a definite advantage given that young men tend to be far more self-confident, willing to argue and, quite simply, louder than their female counterparts. Certainly, it is important to register this concern and to recognize that students who are naturally shy, whatever their gender, can all too easily be marginalized in a lively tutorial discussion. But it would be dangerous to suggest that any of these capabilities could be inherent in only one gender.

Generally, current Oxford students are enthusiastic advocates for tutorial teaching. They value them as a prominent and stimulating part of their course. Initially, the prospect of debate and discussion with expert tutors does seem daunting, and it is only through the on-going cycle of weekly meetings that most have been are able to master the art. But in time students do find them to be an engaging – even exciting – means of developing and expanding their understanding of their subject. If anything the opportunities for wide-ranging discussion and debate have increased in recent years as the formal one-on-one structure of tutorials has been modified. The tutorial in contemporary Oxford has evolved into a dynamic, flexible and popular method of teaching. Perhaps the only (slight) disappointment is that the eccentrics so prominent in the past are now so decidedly thin on the ground.

15. Reflections of an early career-politics Tutor

James Panton, sometime Lecturer in Politics, St John's College

For the early-career academic, teaching tutorials at Oxford can be a daunting task. Tutors know, of course, that they have read more widely, thought more deeply, and, if confident about what they do, had a few more insights about the subject than the students who will sit before them. But they know also that after three or more years writing a doctorate on a theme that may well not even appear on the undergraduate syllabus (or perhaps, as I am at time of writing, they are yet to submit for examination their hundred thousand word contribution to the stock of human knowledge) they may be more than a little bit rusty on extensive areas of the syllabus, and lack confidence, after so much time and effort pursuing a single argument, in their ability as generalists with a broad overview of their discipline.

In facing the first few terms teaching tutorials, the novice tutor knows to expect that in the course of a morning's teaching he or she is likely to face the student who has read the reading list from start to finish (although the fact that the student has not thought very deeply about much of it may become clear only after much discussion), and the student who has become fascinated by a single text on which he/she wishes to expound a great thesis and ask searching questions (almost inevitably, the one text the tutor managed to dose through because it is not a real passion, or it is new addition to the syllabus that the tutor is only half-way through, and not sure what much of it means). The new tutor will also face the cocky student who knows everything there is to be known (and who will much like to hear the sound of his (maybe her) own voice as he seeks to prove this fact), and a number of insecure nervous students who know far more than they think they know (but they are not quite sure how, or are not yet confident enough, to say it). Moreover, the tutor knows to expect the good bluffer, who has done little work, but will express a confident opinion on any topic; and from time to time, he or she will encounter the truly exceptional student who, to the novice tutor, is likely to seem far more naturally gifted than this early-career tutor actually feels.

In time, the confidence grows (to admit that one doesn't know the answer to the question, or hasn't read that particular book in quite some time), and experience develops (to spot the work-shy bluffer from the brilliant, the shy and insecure student from the lazy or the uninspired). And with that confidence and experience comes the realization that the very features of tutorial teaching that made it such a daunting endeavour at the outset – that every tutorial, even on the same essay question, will be different; that every student has different passions and gets excited by different aspects of the course, often the very aspects the tutor feels they understand least; and inevitably, each of those students may need a different approach to draw out their thinking and encourage their understanding – these aspects are precisely what makes tutorial teaching such a special and rewarding task. Tutorial teaching is rarely easy, almost always intellectually exhausting. But when it works, it is an intellectually exciting, often exhilarating, way to spend a morning.

Many contributors to this book have stressed the egalitarian nature of the tutorial relationship between academic and student. It is also a peculiar relationship that contains at its core a creative tension. The tutor certainly has read and thought a bit more and for a bit longer about the subject; but bright students will quickly see through cynical attempts to hide one's ignorance or uncertainty, and they will be put off by attempts to bluff through answers to tricky or searching questions. The fundamentally egalitarian nature of the relationship is set from the outset by the fact that, unlike in primary or secondary education, the tutor is not a teacher who is there to answer questions, much less to give the *right* answer. On the contrary, the tutor is a (perhaps only slightly) older, definitely a little bit more experienced, but fundamentally similar kind of individual seeking answers to difficult and perplexing questions about the world. The role of the tutor, in as much as it can be generalized, is perhaps only to act as a guide who can frame questions, and encourage the student to frame questions, in a way that will allow for further, fruitful, intellectual pursuit. The role of tutors is to welcome and guide students into an area of knowledge about which they have a passion, and about which they may have many well developed ideas, but the good tutor is well aware of the fact that the student has as much potential to contribute to development of knowledge and understanding as they do themselves. At the beginning of a tutorial tutors will probably have a sense of where they want to get to at the end of the hour; in a reasonably successful tutorial, they may well have got there. But if the tutorial has really worked, chances are both tutor and student will have ended up somewhere else entirely; and both may be all the better for the experience.

Such brilliant tutorials are possible precisely because of the informal and flexible nature of student-tutor relationship. The relationship is collaborative, exploratory, and intellectually challenging. But there are contradictory pressures in contemporary academic culture that, if we fail to guard against them both as tutors and as students, might very well serve to erode that open-ended informality upon which good tutorial teaching is based. I want to suggest three lines of thinking, common in contemporary culture, that we should all, students and tutors alike, reject.

The first problematic line of thinking:
Unlike those glory days where university in general, Oxbridge in particular, was a place where the intellectual elite could train the next generation of social elite, and so both tutors and students knew what was expected, why they were there, and what the rules of the game were, the modern university system has the task of taking young people from a host of different class, educational and experience backgrounds, and putting them all through a common education system. The problematic idea is that many modern kids are not really up to the task. This is an idea that floats around behind the scenes, and in particular, when we turn our thoughts to working-class kids and young people from what are euphemistically called 'non-traditional' backgrounds.

On this view, the expectation that students might turn out one, perhaps two, essays in a week, is seen as implicitly privileging those already over-privileged public school kids who have been well-coached in the black arts of essay writing and bluffing.

Those from different backgrounds will inevitably feel alienated, become disenchanted, and ultimately loose out, in a system that was established historically to train the social elite. Expecting students to produce such a quantity of work in such a short time is criticized for leaving them far too little time for reflection at best, or for inevitably leading them to panic and despair, at worst. On this view weekly or twice-weekly tutorials – in which students have no place to hide their ignorance (whether they failed to grasp the material or failed to do enough work), and in which the key advantage over other teaching structures is the possibility of putting students under serious and sustained intellectual pressure to develop, expound and defend their ideas – are seen as little more than sites for intellectual bullying, piling on unnecessary and unhelpful stress that is most likely to lead students towards depression, low-self esteem, even self-harm or suicide! You may accuse me of exaggerating to make my point, but a quick survey of the educational press will reveal copious examples of all these arguments (to give but three examples, look at Currie, 2000; Sanders, 2003; and Winter, 2003).

I have argued elsewhere (Panton, 2004) that this vision of students is not only patronising, but that it can only result in giving students a much diminished educational experience which ends up selling them short. Others have begun to make an important challenge to the increasingly therapeutic turn within education (see, for example: Ecclestone & Hayes, 2008) that understands students in terms of their potential vulnerability rather than their potential for engagement and development. The important point I wish to make here is a straightforward enough one: the expectations we have of our students are one of the most important signals for students themselves of what they might be capable of. If we think there was something problematic in the exclusive and elitist system of old, we have a funny way of challenging the problem if we begin from the assumption that the children of the current elite are up to the challenge of a rigorous education, while the children of the 'great unwashed' (a childhood of which I am myself very proud) can only stumble and fall when put under pressure. If we begin from the assumption that students are weak and vulnerable, are likely to be alienated by being put on the spot intellectually, or are likely to buckle under the strain of handing in essays on time, we should not be surprised if our expectations come true. If, by contrast, we begin with the assumption that our students are up to the challenge – and if we encourage students themselves to hunger for the transformative challenge that university education can provide – then we are likely to discover ourselves working with students who exceed our expectations, and who come to demand far more of us as tutors.

There is a lesson for students here as well as tutors: expect to be challenged, and want to be pushed; you will likely discover you are capable of things you never thought possible. As educators, we are by instinct most likely meritocrats. Only if we think young people are up to the challenge, and encourage them to think that themselves, will we create a truly meritocratic education system in which everyone who is prepared to work hard, and who is open to being pushed, is welcome, and likely to thrive.

The second problematic line of thinking:
The second pressure has already been mentioned elsewhere in this volume: that 'an emphasis upon examinations has pervaded the whole of education, from primary level upwards and distorted its meaning' (Probert Smith, Ch 7 of this book). In the increasingly instrumentalised university sector there is a tendency to measure academic quality in terms of the quantity of good degrees achieved by undergraduates (where 'good degrees' means upper-seconds or firsts; no two-twos or thirds will be accepted!). For many departments and institutions prestige and funding, not to mention existential purpose, seem increasingly to depend upon producing a sizeable number of graduates with high-ranking degree marks; and of course, the more good degrees an institution can produce, the more likely it is to attract students.

For early-career tutors there is a temptation to measure the quality of teaching in terms of student results. Implicitly, one can begin to feel a pressure that tutoring is about teaching students to pass exams. In a culture in which students are encouraged to understand university as a necessary stepping stone on route to a career, and in which undergraduate degrees are sold to school leavers on the basis that graduates earn more than non-graduates, it is hardly surprising if some students think tutorials are all about preparation for the achievement of a good 2.1 in Finals. What is more worrying than this, however, is that many young and early-career academics have grown up in exactly the same instrumentalist climate, and face the measure of their quality as tutors in terms of the degrees their students achieve. Implicitly or explicitly, we can succumb to the pressure of teaching for exams; asking interesting questions, or going down the byways and alleyways that come up in tutorial or seminar discussion, becomes a distraction from the job: covering a syllabus that we know the student needs to master in order to get their degree.

Again, there is a lesson, or a word of advice, for both young tutors and incoming students. Exams results are important: they are the measure of what students have achieved, how sophisticated their thinking has become and how far they have pushed and developed their ideas. They are an important, but not necessarily the most important, marker of achievement. And they are a good, if inevitably very often rough, marker of that achievement. But doing well in exams comes from collaborating in the open-ended intellectual relationship – working, reading, questioning and most of all really thinking; exploring different avenues, from time to time being prepared to go off piste, and understanding tutorials as a space for the development of such intellectual freedom and curiosity. The knowledge, the confidence, and the ability to do well, comes from engaging with a subject and pushing your understanding. Tutors are generally very good at that: it is, after all, because they have chosen to devote themselves to pushing their own understanding that they are a tutor in the first place. Tutors are likely to be far less good, tutorials will become far less exciting, and intellectual development far more restricted, if, instead of an intellectual guide welcoming students into a world of higher learning, the tutor is expected to become merely the provider of skills and information: this is what you need to know, these are the important points you need to make, and this is how you need to write your essays if you want to get a 2.1.

The third problematic line of thinking:
The third pressure that contemporary academic culture throws up is one that increasingly sets teaching and research in a false opposition. Most tutors are in the position of being tutors because they have an essential curiosity about the world, and they have devoted themselves to pursuing that curiosity wherever it may lead them, but, almost always, by writing about what they have discovered. From a position in which writing and publishing was an essential means of communicating ideas, we are now in a climate in which writing, especially articles for journal publication, is a quantitative measure of intellectual worth and academic standing.

In order to progress from early-career to tenured academic, I need a publication record of top-quality articles in the top-quality journals, hopefully well-cited by the top-academics in my field. This is the newly instrumentalised measure of my quality as an intellectual and an academic. The open-ended exploration, the intellectual passion and engagement, the shear curiosity and passion to understand that world, that drives all academics in what they do, is still there, but it is mediated in a very instrumentalist way: the quantitative measurement achieved by journal publication. With such a difficult task, and such steep competition in the research field, surely tutorial teaching can only be a distraction? Almost inevitably, research and teaching can begin to conflict, for we are all short of time, and each, it might seem, can only be a distraction from the other. The idea that research-led teaching is core to what we do: that the intellectual engagement we have with students – exploring ideas, pushing back the boundaries of their, and our own, understanding, with all the freedom and spontaneity and detours that might entail – that idea of tutorial teaching runs the risk of being forgotten when on the one hand tutorials are about teaching to exams, and, on the other hand, my intellectual work is a constant striving for publication.

But the solution to this is straightforward: it is, as Alan Ryan hints elsewhere in this book, about recognizing the importance of scholarship. 'The thought that it is impossible to be a good teacher without engaging in cutting edge research is as utterly implausible as the thought that all cutting edge researchers would like to teach', says Ryan: 'what is not implausible is the thought that good scholarship is needed for good teaching' (Ryan, Ch 2 of this book). And I would add, that in attempting to get to grips with the question of what constitutes good scholarship, we might start with the question of what it takes to teach tutorials: to develop one's understanding through research and reading and serious thought, and to attempt to communicate your thinking through collaboration with some of the brightest minds of their generation. It is not the only thing, but it is a very good start.

What is to be done?
None of these three pressures is inevitable, and they may all seem like pretty distant pressures when one sits in Oxford: but the pressures are nonetheless real. And, if we think that one of the most important aspects of pursuing academic work is to challenge and question our own assumptions about the discipline in which we work as much as we challenge those of our peers, we would be wise not to ignore the

assumptions that are sneaking into the discourse of academic life in general, and the role we play as tutors and educators in particular. It would be too easy to look up from our books, or leave our tutorials at the end of the day, and realize the world we live in has changed, perhaps for the worse, but that we failed to notice.

If we come to believe, and encourage our students to believe, that rigorous essays and hours of deep thought (and all the associated pressure that comes with that) are probably beyond their capabilities – and, if with that belief, we come to accept that our role is not as intellectual guides into a world of knowledge and exploration, the boundaries of which are there only to be pushed, but rather that we are facilitators towards good degree marks – then tutorial teaching will inevitably become less exciting, less essential, more of a chore, and without doubt, a distraction from pursuing the publication record that a young academic needs to secure the desired career. It will also become far less engaging and challenging for students.

If, on the contrary, we hold back from falling into these assumptions – if we remember why we became academics and researchers in the first place, what it was about the world that made us desire to understand it, and what it was about those who taught us as undergraduates that filled us with a passion to follow them (or a passion to prove them wrong!) – then we will surely be able to transmit a bit of that passion and understanding and essential curiosity to those we teach in tutorials. And if, as a newly arriving tutorial student, you recognize that the university experience offers you a few short years in which to reflect upon the world, to push ideas and to be pushed in your thinking, then you can join in, and push your tutors to engage in, an intellectually exciting, certainly demanding, but ultimately rewarding experience. Good exam results and increasing choice on the job market are as important to students as are you achieving good results, and their own impressive publication record, to tutors and academics. But it was intellectual curiosity, and the essential search for knowledge and understanding, that brought student and tutor together in the first place. And that is fundamentally what it is all about.

Bibliography:

J Currie (2008) 'Not all in the mind', *The Times Higher Education Supplement*, 28 April.

K Eccleston and D Hayes (2008) *The Dangerous Rise of Therapeutic Education*. Routledge.

James Panton (2004) 'Challenging Students' in D Hayes (ed) *The RoutledgeFalmer Guide to Key Debates in Education*. RoutledgeFalmer.

C Sanders (2003) 'Overworked students suffer lower quality of learning', *The Times Higher Education Supplement*, 20 June.

R Winter (2003) 'Alternative to the essay', *The Guardian*, 10 June.

16. 'Of Studies in a University'
A.H. Smith, sometime Warden, New College

What follows is the text of an Address delivered to New College 'Freshers' in the Chapel on 11th October, 1953, as reprinted from A.H. Smith's *Selected Essays and Addresses* (Basil Blackwell, Oxford, 1963, pp 107-111)...

On this first Sunday of another academic year, which marks for some of you the beginning of your life in the College, I think you might wish to reflect for a short while upon your life and studies here, and on the manner and degree in which they will fit you for work and duties which will be incumbent on you hereafter. For there can be no doubt that the free, happy and privileged life which you lead in this place is a form of training or preparation, and it can only be justified if it fits those who enjoy it for useful service in their later careers whatever they may prove to be.

The training or preparation presumably has the aim of enabling you to give to the world something which it needs. I think therefore we may begin by considering some needs (prima facie relevant to our enquiry) of our civilization to-day, and then ask whether those who have received a university training, and more particularly the traditional training of this university, seem especially fitted to supply them. If we approach the question in this way, it is evident that there are needed skills and forms of knowledge demanding intelligence of a high order and the capacity for prolonged thinking. I have in mind the various branches of science, or mathematics or medicine. Those who c are trained in them at the university may pursue them for the rest of their lives, either in their more or less direct application to practical ends or in pure research which often is determined by no external goal but springs straight from the mind's innate desire to know and to understand. Of course mankind welcomes all that it can obtain in the development and application of science. It has come to accept also and to esteem the work of those who search (as in the abstract and seemingly profitless pursuit of mathematics) after knowledge for its own sake; for it has learnt that their lonely speculations may be instruments which in the end have the power to transform the world. All these are plainly in themselves beneficent activities for which the university should and does afford the necessary training.

So far general opinion would concur in its judgement of what our civilization needs and universities should provide. There is not, I think, an equal readiness to accept as necessary the kind of lonely and purposeless inquiry of which I have spoken in other fields than those of science or mathematics. Many will be sceptical about the worth of prolonged and laborious inquiry in subjects such as remote periods of history or literature of languages which are new dead. Some, however, might be persuaded by argument that this spirit of inquiry and of single-minded search for truth is something so precious that it should be encouraged in any field of learning which men are eager to investigate. I for my part would indeed wish you to believe in the great worth of this temper of mind, and I am sure that the encouragement of it is an aim which any system of university education should steadily pursue.

Some of you will in your later life be engaged in the fields of work of which I have spoken, as practitioners, or researchers, but, perhaps only a minority. Of the rest there are some who will be entering professions such as those connected with the law or with school-teaching, while others will be involved in some of the many forms of administration or business. In the latter case your studies here do not seem designed to give you any special equipment which you will need; and even in the other case of the professions which I have mentioned, the connection between your studies and the work which you will do hardly seems so close as it might be, since the studies constantly diverge from practical application or at least go beyond what is needed in practice. Is there here some failure of adjustment between university training and the business of the world?

We shall come perhaps to the heart of the matter if we ask whether there is some temper of mind, hard to come by in the confusion, pressure and excitement of the world's business, which yet the world needs. If we frame this question, does it not seem that what is perhaps most to be desired in our day is that which is hardest to obtain? For that of which I am thinking is the detachment and quiet of mind untroubled by recurrent anxieties and having instead the sense of an inner security, a spirit and temper in which a man, without the bias which comes from fear or the craving for favour, seeks patiently to understand the bewildering problems with which, in the world as it is, he is continually confronted, and to solve them to the best of his powers in all sincerity, soberness and truth. I would not deny (for it would be useless) that in the business of the world time and leisure which are needed for the exercise of such a temper cannot always be compassed; nor again would I deny that compromise must constantly be made between what is best and what is practical. For the most part in all probability a man must be content with imperfectly considered judgements and hasty action. But it makes a world of difference if, having learnt to follow high and exacting standards and bowing only to necessity, he knows imperfection for what it is, and never takes it for the best.

None can deny or belittle the value of such a temper in the affairs of men, or measure the influence of one who has it. I want now to suggest that having considered it we can see more clearly the aim and value of much in your studies about which we were dubious before. We noticed how many of them were concerned with the prolonged investigation of matters which seemed to have little reference to the problems which confront our civilization; and yet it was with these problems that either directly or through their repercussions you were bound at one time or another to be involved. When everywhere (so it seemed) there were countless and urgent problems, could a university legitimately practise so great a detachment from them that it encouraged and promoted the patient examination of such subjects as he ancient classics or far-off periods of history or the laborious and remote investigations of philosophy? There are some who would minimize the remoteness and detachment of these studies and would contend that they have many connections with the problems of the present. I would not wish to say that there was no justification for this line of thought. But in the context of our present reflections, where we have begun to think of these remote studies in relation to the habit of mind which we have commended, perhaps even their detachment is a part of their value, and indispensable to the aim which they serve.

Let me put more clearly the point which we are considering. We saw how difficult it would be in the actual business of the world, where there is haste and anxiety and every kind of bias, to learn the habit of calm consideration and serene judgement. But in the detachment your studies in this place you can learn it. For they are studies attended by no initial bias of the mind nor by anxiety to find at all costs a solution on which immediate action can be taken. They offer small opportunity to the influence of fashion or popular acclaim. In following them there can be learnt patience and perseverance and the determination to understand the nature of a problem and the conditions necessary for its solution. And they inculcate integrity of mind and an unswerving regard for truth. I do not think that we can doubt the rightness of the aim which underlies our studies or the service which its fulfilment would be to mankind.

You may have observed that in my description of the temper of mind which we have been considering I have included two elements which seem to be disparate and separable. On the one- hand I have referred, in relation to the studies in which a man is engaged, to the search for truth and the desire to understand, fully and patiently, the problems which he finds involved. On the other hand I have spoken of steadiness of mind, of the sense of quiet and inner security, and of freedom from preoccupation with other cares. Now we can see, I think, that the two elements are connected. For at least it is clear that patient study needs as its condition freedom from disturbing cares and the anxiety which they bring. But I would go further and say that patient study and the search for truth, if we try them, will be found to create their own condition. Nor is it difficult to give the reason for this. For eager and dispassionate study involves preoccupation with the search and not at all with the searcher; and it is in self-forget-fulness that there is always release from anxiety. The themes of which I have spoken are in no chance conjunction, and you will find in your experience that they are continually crossing. You have other aids besides your studies to the attainment of a quiet and secure temper of mind. I would count as such the sense of security which comes from membership of a society united in a common purpose; or the opportunities you have both for secluded study and for a happy life with your fellows; or again the sense which you may gain in your life here of a long tradition with its visible embodiment everywhere in the buildings of your College. In all these things, if you reflect on them, you will see connections with the themes of which we have been thinking, and you will find in practice that they are no small aid to that happy and stable temper which I would have you seek.

Do I seem to have given in your Chapel tonight a purely secular address? I do not think that the temper of mind of which I have been speaking is far from the borders of religion, if indeed religion has any borders. But I will add one word more. Bear in mind what I have sad about the element of self- forgetfulness in the crossing themes, and ask yourselves whether in religion there may not be found in particular a kind of self-forgetfulness which nothing else can afford. Perhaps at the least many of you will feel, as I do, that it would seem to be the consummation of our aims and purposes in this College if we believed that they were part of an eternal purpose in which we were ourselves absorbed, so that, reflecting on all the busy play of our life here, our minds would be filled in the act of contemplation with the sense of an ultimate and inviolable security.

PREFACE TO THE CHINESE EDITION, 2008

When I was approached about the possibility of a Chinese translation and publication by Peking University Press of *The Oxford Tutorial* I asked myself whether it might be that the development of the Socratic tradition in teaching and learning that underpins the pedagogical philosophy of the Oxford tutorial (see Chapter 6) had also evolved independently in Eastern culture and philosophy as it had from Ancient Greece through the Western philosophical tradition. I have never studied philosophy, still less comparative philosophy, but I was intrigued that, whilst attending the Beijing Forum 2007 with an invitation from Peking University to give a Paper on liberal education and the Oxford tutorial, I had come across a Paper given by Richard Bosley (University of Alberta, Canada) on 'The Doctrine of the Mean East and West' that explored the parallel development of the Mean in Eastern philosophy (via Confucius, Mengzi and Xunzi) and at around the same time but separately in Western philosophy (via Pythagoros, Plato and Aristotle). Bosley comments: 'The doctrine of the Mean represents one of the most striking examples of parallel intellectual development in more than 2000 years of written philosophy'.

I was also conscious of how in many religions and cultures much the same code of social behaviour has evolved in seemingly unconnected ways; a rather useful guide to daily life that amounts to, do to others only what you would want them to do to you. Thus, in Christianity there is 'as ye would that men should do to you, do ye also to them likewise'; in Judaism, 'love thy neighbour as thyself'; in Confucianism, 'do not inflict on others what you yourself would not wish done to you'. Similarly, in Islam we have: 'no one of you is a believer until he desires for his brother that which he desires for himself'; while in Hinduism there is: 'one should not behave towards others in a way which is disagreeable to oneself'. In Buddhism we find: 'hurt not others in a way you would find hurtful'; and, finally, from the Ancient Greek philosophers: 'do not do to others that which would anger you if others did it to you' (Socrates) and 'may I do to others as I would that they would do unto me' (Plato). The overlap in wording between Socrates (469-399 BC) and Confucius (551-479 BC), each as quoted above, is, of course, especially interesting, and hence I bought myself a copy of Confucius, *The Analects* (translated by Raymond Dawson in the 'Oxford World's Classics' series and published by Oxford University Press in 1993). Incidentally, the *Encyclopedia Britannica* entry for Confucius comments to the effect that *The Analects* 'capture Confucian spirit in form and content in the same way that the Platonic dialogues embody Socratic pedagogy'...

While heeding Dawson's wise warning that one should be careful not to read too easily into Confucius too much from one's own 'heavy baggage of preconceptions which derive ultimately from Western philosophical and religious beliefs', it was striking, to my very untutored mind, that Confucius uses terms that are echoed in Newman's 'The Idea of a University' (1852) as itself perhaps the most complete statement of liberal education (see Chapter 1). Newman's most famous sentences on liberal education are probably as now set out in this paragraph and the next two: 'The process of training, by which the intellect... is disciplined for its own sake, for the perception of its own proper object, and for its own highest culture, is called Liberal Education... And to set forth the right standard, and to train according to it, and to help forward all students towards it according to their various capacities, this I conceive to be the business of a University'. Moreover, this process creates 'the gentleman' with 'a cultivated intellect, a delicate taste, a candid, equitable, dispassionate mind, a noble and courteous bearing on the conduct of life – these are the connatural qualities of a large knowledge; they are the objects of a University'.

Thus, through Liberal Education: 'A habit of mind is formed which lasts through life, of which the attributes are freedom, equitableness, calmness, moderation, and wisdom... [what] I have ventured to call a philosophical habit'. Newman resists the petty-minded idea, peddled then as now, that 'Education should be confined to some particular and narrow end, and should issue in some definitive work, which can be weighed and measured', where it has to be 'useful', to have 'utility. Newman is concerned that some find it impossible to see 'the real worth in the market of the article called "a liberal education" on the supposition that it does not teach us definitively how to advance our manufactures...' (in modern terms, it seems to have no immediately assessable contribution to the 'learning and skills' agenda, to 'the Knowledge Economy'). He declares, 'I say that a cultivated intellect, because if is a good in itself, brings with it a power and a grace to every work and occupation which it undertakes, and enables us to be more useful...'.

Finally, Newman comments: 'a University training is the great ordinary means to a great but ordinary end; it aims at raising the intellectual tone of society, at cultivating the public mind, at purifying the national taste, at supplying true principles to popular enthusiasm and fixed aims to popular aspiration, at giving enlargement and sobriety to the ideas of the age... It teaches [the student as the educated 'gentleman'] to see things as they are, to go right to the point, to disentangle a skein of thought, to detect what is sophisticated, and to discard what is irrelevant... It shows him how to accommodate himself to others, how to throw himself in their state of mind, how to bring before them his own, how to influence them, how to come to an understanding with them, how to bear with them...' Thus, for Newman the essence of the liberal education is the development of the mind and lodging within it the intellectual virtues that discipline the mind: intellectual integrity, intellectual empathy, and intellectual confidence balanced by intellectual humility and intellectual fair-mindedness.

It is interesting, therefore, that *junzi in* Confucius is translated by Dawson as 'gentleman' (by others as sometimes 'the superior man', 'the noble man', or 'the exemplary man'); *xian* as men of 'virtue and ability', as 'men of quality'; and *shi* as 'scholar-gentleman'. Delving into the text of *The Analects* it seemed to me that there *may* be overlapping Socratic and Confucian concepts: Book 2, item 9, refers to the Master (Master Kong or Kongfuzi as alternative names for Confucius) as having spent 'the whole day talking with Hui' as his favourite pupil, but being disappointed that he did not demonstrate (as Dawson comments) 'sufficient independence of mind for the Master's taste' in that he failed (words from item 9) 'to put any counter-arguments'. In item 12 just below Confucius says: 'A gentleman does not behave as an implement'; and Dawson notes that 'this important saying puts in a nutshell the belief that the gentleman's training should not be confined to particular skills so that he may become the tool or implement of others', thereby reminding us of Newman's emphasis on the value of liberal education as creating independence of mind.

Let me list a few more such seemingly Socratic or Newmanesque thoughts from the Master (and also the reader should compare these with the comments of various authors on liberal education set out in Chapter 1): 'The gentleman has universal sympathies and is not partisan. The small man is partisan and does not have universal sympathies' (2: 14); 'If one studies but does not think, one is caught in a trap. If one thinks but does not study, one is in peril' (2: 15); 'In his attitude to the world the gentleman has no antagonisms and no favouritisms. What is right he sides with' (4: 10); 'To those who are not eager to learn I do not explain anything, and to those who are not bursting to speak I do not reveal anything. If I raise one angle and they do not come back with the other three angles, I will not repeat myself' (7: 8); 'The gentleman is calm and peaceful, the small man is always emotional' (7: 37); '…I hammer at both sides of the question and go into it thoroughly' (9: 8); 'The gentleman, although he behaves in a conciliatory manner, does not make his views coincide with those of others…' (13: 23); 'There are nine things the gentleman concentrates on – in seeing he concentrates on clarity, in listening he concentrates on acuteness… when he is in doubt he concentrates on asking questions…' (16: 10); 'If one studies widely and is sincere in one's purpose, and if one enquires earnestly and reflects on what is at hand, then humaneness is to be found among such activities' (19: 6; in fact, cited as from the Master's disciple, Zixia); and, Zixia again in 19: 7, 'The various craftsmen occupy workshops in order to complete their tasks, but the gentleman studies in order to develop his Way' ('The Way', *dao*, being translated by Dawson as 'the ideal course of conduct for an individual' as 'the Way of the gentleman').

In short, having dipped into *The Analects* I worried even more whether I was indeed reading into Confucius, and despite Dawson's warning, far too much from my own Western philosophical 'baggage'. Or, on the other hand, perhaps there is indeed in Chinese intellectual and cultural history some equivalent of the concept of liberal education as a process of the inculcation within students of the vital life-long skill of critical-thinking and independence of mind as the very essence of what is 'higher' about higher education and of what is supposed to go on in a university as opposed to the aim and form of education in the pre-university, school phase (see the discussion of higher education, liberal education, critical-thinking, academic discourse, and the style of the Oxford tutorial in Chapter 1). At this point I called in the help of experts, of distinguished comparative philosophers in both Cambridge University and Oxford University, who kindly offered me very helpful guidance (and, in the tradition of the Oxford tutorial, a reading list!).

One colleague also issued a Dawson-style warning to the effect that the questions I was asking myself were 'extremely difficult to answer without falling into gross over-simplification, anachronism, condescension or all three'. He felt that 'Socrates would strike a Chinese reader as far more aggressive' than the Confucian style of engaging other masters and his own pupils in dialogue, and that the Chinese emphasis would be 'to make points that are open-ended, implicit, rather than conclusions reached inexorably by the demonstrative methods of argument'. That said, all should agree that the value of liberal education is the encouragement of critical-thinking, and that critical-thinking is more than mere argumentation and disputation for its own sake. Such intellectual activity does, however, foster intellectual engagement, and it is this participation in the academic discourse that develops critical-thinking so that the individual does not fall victim to the arbitrary, the capricious, and the irrational in thinking and ideas.

As part of my, as it were, tutorial reading, I also referred to two fascinating books: *Ancient Worlds, Modern Reflections: Philosophical Perspectives on Greek and Chinese Science and Culture* (Oxford University Press, 2004) and *The Way and the Word: Science and Medicine in Early China and Greece* (Yale University Press, 2002). The former is by Geoffrey Lloyd (Emeritus Professor of Ancient Philosophy and Science, University of Cambridge), and the latter by Geoffrey Lloyd and Nathan Sivin (Professor of Chinese Culture, University of Pennsylvania). Lloyd & Sivin, in studying China and Greece between c400BC to c200AD, comment that 'by fortunate accident' both 'Greece and China evolved comparably elaborate cultures' where people in both societies 'were not content simply to accept, as the last word, the set of beliefs that tradition or convention handed down'. Yet such 'ancient inquiries did not all follow the same pattern' in that each shared 'a desire to increase understanding but had different ideas about how to go about it'. With respect to Chinese higher education in this period they note that 'studying meant memorizing classics of great length' where within the Grand Academy dominant 'attitudes and modes of conformity were preparation for the education of a bureaucrat, not of an innovator'. This was not least because the concept of 'discussion as impersonal and disinterested, in the fashion to which Greeks aspired, was practically impossible in China' since others saw 'an attack on an idea as an attack on its spokesman' (or 'lineage of masters') and since also 'the teacher-student relationship required deference to the teacher' within 'the highly ritualized character of teacher-pupil relations'.

Thus, Lloyd & Sivin note that the Chinese, unlike the Greeks, emphasized 'classics, canons, or memorials' that reflect 'the general desire for an orthodoxy' and where perhaps 'argument' in academic discourse would be more 'muted', or 'indirect', than in the Western tradition, there being 'no record of public philosophical arguments in ancient China' as recorded in Greece. In short: 'Not many Chinese intellectuals were attracted to open conflict of any kind' in the context of 'disapproval of free intellectual exploration' when such argument was simply 'not a pervasive aspect of scholarly life' (in contrast to 'a Greek public free-for-all'!). Only a few masters 'encouraged argument as a teaching tool' given that the overwhelming values of Chinese culture 'stressed harmony and consensus'; hence motivating 'most intellectuals to express rivalry and contention judiciously and indirectly' compared with 'the Greeks' open aggression'. Moreover, the use of dialogue in Chinese philosophy was 'very different from the face-to-face debates in the agora'.

Overall, Lloyd & Sivin conclude that: 'In China there was no tradition of public debate of the kind that was central in the Greek world. Philosophical and scientific argument tended to be written and indirect and was seldom confrontational... The Chinese mirror image of Greek public debate was a tendency to seek agreement and to claim it even when it did not exist.' They compare this 'genteel and impersonal' style of academic discourse in China with the fiercely adversarial style of Greek intellectual exchanges, and especially in Plato's Academy as the start of 'the institutionalization of higher education' that led on to competition through 'bitter and intense' public argument and debate amongst such private entities 'both for pupils and prestige'. Thus, in contrast to China, the Greek schools 'were there not just, and not even primarily, to hand over a body of teaching, let alone a canon of learned texts'; they did not exist 'to hand on and preserve a tradition, nor yet to supply what could pass as an official orthodoxy'.

And, above all, 'the teacher-pupil relationship looks very different in China and in Greece' for 'Greek pupils were too intent on making their own reputations to pay much attention to the idea that they needed to give their teachers unswerving allegiance'. In doing so, they were operating within 'a culture preoccupied by, and highly self-conscious about, argumentative debates of varying types', in a society where there was 'a deep-rooted preoccupation with competitive debate'. Moreover, such 'stridency' in Greek intellectual debate 'ruled out what the Chinese, for their part, learned to praise, namely, the sense of cooperative effort to find the common ground for a consensus.' Thus, 'Chinese philosophy, lacking the competitive abrasiveness that underlay the Greek variety, remained narrower in its range of exploitation and more inclined to seek general agreement on basic issues.' The Greek intellectuals sought to be 'Masters of the Truth'; their Chinese counterparts, 'Possessors of the Way', aiming at being able 'to advise and guide rulers' as fulfilling 'the political ideal of a wise prince ruling benevolently'. The Greeks operated in the vibrant and pluralist marketplace of ideas where 'aggressive innovation' thrived; the Chinese philosophers had the security of being public sector officials within the political status quo. The Greeks had to emphasise pedagogy as 'an essential part of the activities of philosophers and scientists of all types'; in China 'teaching ranked well below official service on the scale of prestige'. The Greeks sought 'demonstration', 'incontrovertibility', 'clarity', 'deductive rigour', and, in doing so, there was 'a zest for disagreement'; the Chinese explored 'correspondences', 'resonances' and 'interconnections' which meant 'a reluctance to confront established positions with radical alternatives'. That said, Lloyd & Sivin add: 'The Greeks were like the Chinese (and unlike most moderns) in that they did not confuse compiling with knowing'!

In Lloyd's book *Ancient Worlds, Modern Reflections*, he asks 'is there a common or a universal logic' underpinning the use of argument as a technique for persuasion in ancient Greece and China. He explores overlaps and divergences, concluding that, while the Greeks relished and deployed 'logical and linguistic categories in debating situations' more than the Chinese, this 'does not reflect a different underlying or implicit formal logic'. He also considers the search for truth, knowledge and objectivity in the two ancient cultures, again seeing the two philosophies as having more in common than not. Next he considers the questioning of established beliefs and received opinions in each ancient society, yet again stressing the similarities over the differences: the latter relating more to the way in which convention and orthodoxy were challenged than whether it happened at all. As for the form or style of intellectual argument, Lloyd suggests that there are differences: the Greeks seeking a holy grail of 'controvertibility' and 'strict demonstration'; the Chinese settling for less certainty. Lloyd considers the university in each culture, noting the great emphasis on debate in the Greek philosophical schools and a lack of orthodoxy that would have 'amazed the Chinese' (their equivalent of the Greek schools being the lineages, *jia*).

The Chinese, as noted earlier from Lloyd and Sivin, put greater emphasis on the preservation of 'the teaching of a master or canonical text' (*jing*): 'the premium was on transmission and preservation, not on criticism' (albeit both scholarly traditions did indeed share a belief in 'the value attached to learning'). The Chinese, however, had public sector higher education institutions that were not matched in Greece (other than perhaps by the Alexandrian Museum). And this State involvement in higher education, comments Lloyd, is 'a mixed blessing' in that the private sector Greek schools, albeit economically vulnerable, 'had much more room for intellectual manoeuvre than their Chinese counterparts': 'The Chinese state institutions provided reliable [financial] support but this was at the price of setting the [intellectual] agenda'. Lloyd wryly adds: 'the obvious problem that remains with us today is that, if you enjoy state subsidies, you are likely to have to forfeit some of your freedom… it takes an enlightened government to see that it is in their own long-term interest to foster critical institutions of higher education'. Moreover, within the groves of academe (West and East) there is always the risk that 'teachers may be far keener to turn out pupils like themselves than to encourage those pupils to branch out and innovate.'

Lloyd concludes that the ancient philosophical schools at Athens and the philosophical lineages of China each, independently, 'set down markers for the fundamentals of what a university education is for': 'to learn about the world we live in… about the diversities of our literature, our philosophers, our art, our music, about our histories and where we have come from, and where, and who, we are today, and finally to practice self-criticism and to be a source of criticism of society, even though we depend on society to support us. That has always been the dilemma of institutions of higher education, and the need for universities to state and defend their role, not as guardians nor just as transmitters of received knowledge, but as critics and as innovators, has never been greater.'

Finally, one more background text: Annping Chin, *Confucius: A Life of Thought and Politics* (2008, Yale University Press)… Chin sees Confucius as exploring ideas such as worth (*xian*), nobleness (*shang*), and virtue (*de*), as well as benevolence (*ren*), the last as a concept that may link to the call of the present Chinese Government for 'harmonious society' (thus, a *renren* is 'a man with the deepest humanity and the noblest of character, [who] represents the alpha example of moral achievement in Confucius' teachings'). She adds, however, that, while these concepts are similar to those examined by Socrates and Plato, in the *Analects* they are not set out as 'philosophers' conversations': 'Opponents were rarely present in these conversations…'. That said, Chin in summing up her interpretation of Confucius' attitude to the process of education comes close, it seems, to describing Liberal Education: 'Education, in his view, must begin and end with the person who seeks to learn. A teacher cannot make it happen… He would say to his best students that not only were they on their own but under certain circumstances they also had to hold their own even at the risk of contradicting him… The best student, he felt, was someone who, on the strength of his clear judgement, could refuse to go along with his teacher… and the right teacher would want his student to break away because he knew that this was all he could do for his student. Confucius accepted this paradox.'

Chin also notes that Confucius uses the word *hui* for 'teach', not *xun* at all and *jiao* only rarely: *hui* is to teach 'by way of imparting light' or throwing light' according to early Chinese dictionaries, and here one is reminded of the Latin phrase within the crest of the University of Oxford: 'Dominus Illuminatio Mea' (where to teach is associated with enlightenment, with illumination, with lighting the mind…). Moreover, in Chin's discussion of Confucius on 'a gentlemanly adroitness' we see an overlap with Newman's gentleman possessing a 'cultivated intellect': she quotes Confucius from the *Analects* as declaring that 'A person who is gentlemanly and adroit is by nature fair-minded and upright, and he is bent on aiming at what is right. He also listens to what others have to say and is observant of their expressions and moods. He is ever-mindful of not being high-handed. Such a man possesses a gentlemanly adroitness.' Otherwise, however, Chin does not herself draw any comparison between Confucius and Newman, nor with Socrates, Plato and indeed any other Western philosopher.

For Western readers seeking more on the recent (post-Mau) rediscovery of Confucious in modern China see D.A. Bell, 2008, *China's New Confucianicsm: Politics and Everyday Life in a Changing Society* – Bell is Professor of Political Philosophy at Tsinghua University in Beijing. On Chinese history see: J. Fenby (2008), *The Penguin History of Modern China: The Fall and Rise of a Great Power, 1850-2008*; and J. Keay (2008), *China: A History*. Another fascinating 2008 book offers the intriguing thesis that it was the arrival of Chinese knowledge in science/technology and in art that sparked the European Renaissance: G. Menzies, *1434:The year a magnificent Chinese fleet sailed to Italy and ignited the Renaissance*. Bell has a Chapter entitled 'A Critique of Critical-Thinking' in which he sets up an imaginary conversation between 'Professor Kong' (Confucius) and a Western-educated

'Professor Hu', and in which there is a section on 'The Methods of Education in the Humanities' (pp 121-127) where they agree that the inculcation of critical-thinking is the objective or end of higher education but disagree over the means of getting there. Professor Kong sees the Socratic Method as too aggressive and harsh a teaching process, potentially giving rise to 'hostility' and to 'intellectual arrogance'; he argues that the student should understand first and only then evaluate ('It can be dangerous to emphasise critical-thinking at an early stage', says Professor Kong citing from his *Analects*: 'Thinking without learning leads to danger').

So, this text is proffered to the Chinese reader with the possibility that it *merely* explores the Western Socratic tradition lying behind the concept of liberal education as the teaching process in the Oxford tutorial, and that all of this *may* be of interest for thinking about the style of teaching and learning in modern China's universities and how they prepare young people for serving Society and the Economy for the decades ahead of them. In this respect I note from material circulated at the 2007 Beijing Forum and relating to the previous Forum that various contributors had referred to the need for Chinese higher education to encourage an 'innovative spirit' amongst its students, by teaching 'in an exploring style' and integrating the 'innov-ative idea' within 'the entire education process' so that students are encouraged 'to think independently' and 'to break away from stale rules'. Similarly, very much echoing the material in Chapter 1, others involved in Chinese higher education and contributing at the Beijing Forum stressed that university 'teaches you how to think, how to analyse, and how to face challenges'; in short, 'universities teach you how to learn'; what matters is that you have learned to think and study'. Another contributor stressed: 'Education is not job training'; while yet another emphasized: 'Skill-training does not make a true university... what makes a university a university is that is different from a vocational school'. (I note also that a 'Google Scholar' search reveals some thirty journal articles in Chinese either specifically on Oxford's tutorial system or generally on the tutorial as a means of teaching under-graduates.)

In this context of China thinking about the nature and process of its higher education, this little book is offered to the Chinese, as possessors of a great and historic culture, but it is offered also with due humility and only as an example of how teaching takes place in one world-class university. That said, it could just be that this text explores a concept of education that has intriguing historic parallels (and significant differ-ences) within the ancient philosophical traditions of both the West and the East centering on Socrates and Confucius respectively... And this text certainly celebrates the tradition of higher education as developing critical-thinking through academic discourse, of the modern university (as described by Professor Lloyd above) evolving from both the ancient philosophical schools at Athens and also from the philosophical lineages of ancient China. So, let me end this Preface with one further quote from Professor Lloyd's *Ancient Worlds, Modern Reflections*: 'our institutions of higher education would do well to regain some of the strategic ambitions that animated their predecessors before the rise of narrowly utilitarian, vocational, training. Universities have a special responsibility for criticism and they should not be afraid to stand up for the values of pure, disinterested, research.'

And, above all, in relation to students attending such centres of criticism, the liberal education process must broaden their intellectual horizons, must disturb them intellectually, must unsettle and influence them, must get them thinking long and hard, and so eventually must engender a disciplined independence of mind that comes from the development of intellectual integrity and confidence balanced by intellectual humility and fair-mindedness.

Finally, this Chinese edition is dedicated to greater mutual understanding and harmony between the PRC and the UK. It is especially pleasing to be able to make this Dedication at a time when there is ever-growing interest in the history and culture of China, and in a year (2008) when the 60th anniversary lectures in the BBC's prestigious annual Reith Lectures series have been given by Professor Spence of Yale University on China: his first lecture (14th May) was entitled 'Confucian Ways' and in it Professor Spence notes of Confucius that he possessed 'an ongoing patience with the hasty questions of the young' and also 'determination to help them think rather than force their adherence to a particular view'. The Oxford Tutor, when encountering the young students of Oxford University some 2500 years later in 'The Oxford Tutorial', seeks to emulate Confucius by also displaying such patience and determination!

David Palfreyman, New College, University of Oxford (2008)

N.B. The China reader may understandably be confused over the name of my Oxford college, and over the nature of Oxford University as a collegiate university (like the University of Cambridge). The University of Oxford began in the early thirteenth century and is itself a legal entity, along with some 40 independent colleges. Together all these corporate bodies make up the federal or collegiate university, the colleges with the main task of teaching undergraduate students and the University's academic departments with the main task of teaching postgraduate students and doing academic research. The Oxford student is a 'Junior Member' both of the University and also of his/her College (and indeed most academics/faculty are senior members/employees both of the University as a Lecturer and also of a College as a Tutorial Fellow). New College is one of the oldest, grandest and wealthiest Oxford colleges, founded over 600 years ago in 1379 (when it was then 'new'!), and still occupying its original buildings (see www.new.ox.ac.uk). The full, formal name of the College is 'Saint Mary College of Winchester in Oxenford', but, back in the 1380s (as now), it was much easier to refer to the 'New College'! New College teaches some 400 undergraduate students in all academic subjects, and also has about 200 graduate students as Members of the College. Overall the University has some 11,000 undergraduates and 6,000 graduate students, of which c750 are from China and Hong Kong (the second largest group of overseas students after Americans at c1500). For more on the Oxford collegiate system see Tapper & Palfreyman, *Oxford and the Decline of the Collegiate Tradition* (2000; second edition due 2009).

The China reader may also be interested to know more about Socrates, given the mention throughout this book of the Socratic Method of teaching (and especially in Chapter 6 by Robin Lane Fox). A quick look at any encyclopedia tells us that Socrates (c469-399BC) was a Greek philosopher whose work has not survived directly but only indirectly via 'the Socratic dialogues' (conversations, speeches) from such a disciple as the historian Xenophon (c430-c355BC) and notably from his favourite pupil the philosopher Plato (c428-347BC), who was himself the teacher of Aristotle (384-322BC) and the founder of the Athenian Academy as a kind of university or school of philosophy. The Socratic Method was employed to question and challenge conventional wisdom and assumptions; it is often defined as something like a means of reaching truth by carefully questioning, and then in turn criticizing the answers received: a question and answer session – even tutorial - that the Greeks labeled 'elenchus'. Brief and readable introductions to these key Western thinkers are C.C.W. Taylor on Socrates (1998) and J. Annas on Plato (2003) in the Oxford University Press series 'A Very Short Introduction'. The former comments: 'virtually everyone whose business is teaching finds some affinity with the Socratic method of challenging the student to examine his or her beliefs, to revise them in the light of argument, and to arrive at answers through critical reflection on the information presented'. It is from Plato that we get the famous concept of Socrates comparing himself to a midwife in terms of bringing forth, and testing, the ideas of those he taught or conversed with: 'This at least is true of me as well as of midwives... the god compels me to be a midwife... Take people who associate with me... At first some of them seem quite stupid, but as the association goes on all of them to whom the god grants it turn out to make amazing progress... they have never learned anything from me; rather they have discovered within themselves many fine things, and brought them to birth. And for the delivery the god and myself are responsible' ('Thaetetus', 150 c-d). One is reminded of the equally ancient Chinese philosopher, Lao Tzu, who commented that 'of the best teachers the students say that "We did it all ourselves"...'. For more on Ancient Greece generally see Robin Lane Fox, *The Classical World: An Epic History from Homer to Hadrian* (2006); and for more on Western ancient philosophy see Anthony Kenny, *A New History of Western Philosophy: Volume 1, Ancient Philosophy* (2004).

A Note on OxCHEPS

OxCHEPS, as the **Ox**ford Centre for **H**igher **E**ducation **P**olicy **S**tudies, is privately funded, is directed by David Palfreyman, and is based at New College, Oxford, OX1 3BN, UK (web-address http://oxcheps.new.ox.ac.uk/).

The OxCHEPS mission statement is:

> *To improve understanding of higher education by challenging existing thinking and received wisdom in higher education policy-making; and, on the basis of a rigorous programme of applied comparative research and consultancy successfully linking theory and practice in higher education, to generate an informed debate on topical higher education issues.*

The English language text of this book can be down-loaded from the 'Papers' page of the OxCHEPS website, which also offers the 'HE Law Casebook' and the 'Law Updates' service in support of Farrington & Palfreyman (2006), *The Law of Higher Education* (Oxford University Press). In addition, the 12 volume Taylor & Francis/Routledge *International Studies in Higher Education* series is detailed on its own page at the website, while the 17 volume Open University Press/McGraw-Hill *Managing Universities & Colleges* series is listed under the 'Resources' page.

A Note on obtaining this book, in-print and on-line

This book can be obtained in print from Blackwell's Bookshop, Broad Street, Oxford (01865 792792, Education Department); and also from Blackwell's Online (www.blackwell.co.uk) or Amazon: the book is *not* available directly from OxCHEPS, other than as an electronic version via its web-site at the Papers page. The Chinese translation is published by Peking University Press, Beijing, PRC.

*Ox*CHEPS

BLACKWELL

ALDEN